Out of the Shadows

A Memoir

RACHEL ROSEBUD

Copyright @2021 by Rachel Rosebud

All rights reserved. No part of this book may be reproduced in any form or by any electronic or mechanical means, including information storage and retrieval systems, without permission in writing from the publisher, except by reviewers, who may quote brief passages in a review.

This publication contains the opinions and ideas of its author. It is intended to provide helpful and informative material on the subjects addressed in the publication. The author and publisher specifically disclaim all responsibility for any liability, loss or risk, personal or otherwise, which is incurred as a consequence, directly or indirectly, of the use and application of any of the contents of this book.

WORKBOOK PRESS LLC
187 E Warm Springs Rd,
Suite B285, Las Vegas, NV 89119, USA

Website: https://workbookpress.com/
Hotline: 1-888-818-4856
Email: admin@workbookpress.com

Ordering Information:
Quantity sales. Special discounts are available on quantity purchases by corporations, associations, and others. For details, contact the publisher at the address above.

Library of Congress Control Number:
ISBN-13:   978-1-955459-69-3 (Paperback Version)
           978-1-955459-64-8 (Digital Version)

REV. DATE: 05.06.2021

Contents

Introduction 07

PART 1

1
The Early Years 09

2
New Developments 14

3
A New Start 17

4
The Mental Ward 20

5
Home Again 26

6
Divorce 29

7
The Mental Hospital Again 31

8
On the Road Again 35

9
Home Again 37

10
Locked Up 41

11
The Residential Treatment Center 44

12
On the Road Again 46

13
Booking It Again 50

PART 2

14
New Life 56

15
New Beginnings At Home 62

16
Working 67

17
Romance 71

18
Down South 79

19
Who Am I, Anyway? 87

20
Independence and Freedom 92

21
Romance Again 101

22
Eye Openers 106

23
Choices 109

24
Growing Up 114

25
A New Family 121

26
Good-bye 128

Introduction

I'd like to start by saying this is a story and it happens to be a true story. I look back on my life and recollect many things, some good, some not so good. As I wrote this book I found things out about myself as I just said some good some not so good. But life goes on. I'm hoping that this book will help you in your journey of life.

Needless to say I changed the names throughout this book to protect the innocent and the not so innocent. There are those who may recognize themselves in this book in different ways. So take this to heart. Writing this wasn't easy since I had to write the whole book from the beginning so it would be in the format the publishers wanted. There were portions that were written differently and I believe there were reasons for that, I don't know for sure but I trust things will be just like it's supposed to be.

Hope you enjoy this book.

PART 1

1
The Early Years

"Daddy, wait for me." We were at church and going to the educational building down the hill. I wanted to keep up with my daddy. I looked down and saw his footsteps in the mud and matched mine in his, my feet pointed slightly outward just as his were. This man was so special to me. He was my hero.

One day, we were going to the store together. Boy, was I lucky, as it was just the two of us. That's saying something, since there were five children in my family. I was next to the youngest. When Daddy was paying, the man behind the counter commented that I was a cute little boy. Daddy just beamed and patted me on the head.

Wait, I thought, *I'm not a boy. I'm your little girl.* Did he have any idea how that made me feel? Did Daddy know how much I idolized him and wanted more than anything to please him? Not long after this incident, Daddy didn't seem to think of me as his special one in the family anymore. It seemed that all of a sudden Douglas, my younger brother, had taken that special place of number one in Daddy's life. We all knew that he was Daddy's pet.

What had I done wrong? Was it because I wasn't a

boy? From that day on, I never felt accepted for who I was. There were even times when I was in the bathroom by myself and tried to urinate using an empty toilet paper roll, pretending to be a boy.

My sense of rejection began at a very early age—at five or six. I don't remember exactly when. From that moment, I never felt loved, nor did I feel worthy of love. Why didn't my hero, whom I loved so much, not love me anymore? I was sure he would rather that I be a boy.

When school started, those feelings went along with me. I was an outcast; I never felt a part of anything, nor can I remember having friends. But somewhere deep within me I had a longing to be accepted and loved for who I was. Unfortunately, I felt I had to earn that love. I would do anything to be accepted and liked. Thus a performance-oriented love search began.

Many children do things to get attention: get good grades, be good at sports, etc. Well, there is another way to get attention, albeit negative attention: act up. At one point in elementary school, I found the other misfits, and we acted up, driving the teachers crazy. In sixth grade, I took the route of becoming the teacher's pet; he filled the father role that was lost to me. I became a straight-A student, and he gave me special attention.

Meanwhile, at home, things were pretty bad. It wasn't just my own unhappiness. Mom and Dad had five children in seven years. Mom was nineteen when the first of us was born and twenty-six at number five. She had married my father at eighteen, hoping to leave an unhappy home herself. She met him when he was in New Orleans attending the New Orleans Baptist Seminary.

He had felt called to be in the ministry and was going to the seminary. She wanted to become a missionary. He was twenty-seven; she was seventeen. My grandmother used to joke that my father was teaching my mom. They got married right after she graduated from high school.

All those babies, responsibilities, and just trying to survive took quite a toll on their lives. My father did some preaching as we grew up, but he never had a full-time church job— just short periods, since he'd always have another a full-time job. For a time, Dad tried to preach every weekend at a church forty minutes away. It was there, while listening to him preach one Sunday morning, that I asked Jesus Christ to come into my life. I was ten. Douglas did too.

But that part of our life was a farce, since Mom had really lost it. She had been drinking for a while, getting her booze from men at work who would it off. At times Mom would mix her drinking with the numerous drugs she had been prescribed. One time Dad gathered up all of her drugs in a shoebox and hid them. It was so bad that she overdosed once and had to be taken to have her stomach pumped at the hospital.

It seemed our lives were falling apart around us. Dad still worked full time and tried hard to keep the family together. Mom worked full time too. Mom did all the laundry, and Dad did the cooking. On weekends, when Mom did the laundry, she would go outside and hang up the clothes while falling-down drunk. This didn't affect me as much as my older siblings. Eric, the oldest, was ashamed. He found his way of escaping by becoming totally engrossed in Boy Scouts. He stayed in Scouts for years and withdrew from the rest of the family. He remains so to this day.

Afraid that I would tell Dad, Mom offered me some of the beer so that I wouldn't tell. I want to add a note about my first taste of beer, or whatever it was, since my mom told me she never drank beer. It was booze of some sort, but you don't give such things to a child. My mom was so broken, and it makes me cry as I write about this. But life goes on, albeit in strange ways indeed.

Our family was so full of it. Peter, who was the brother older than me, got into a lot trouble. He vandalized one of the local schools with some friends—if you want to call them that. He also ran away several times. Briana ended up in the local mental hospital at age thirteen. Poor Briana. She'd had a lot of things dumped on her. She tried so hard to take up the slack and keep the house clean. I'm amazed that our family actually lived through the many things thrown at us. It was like some crazy movie.

Our home life centered on TV. We would gather around it and vegetate as much as we could in those days, when more wholesome stuff was available. Mom would lie on the sofa, and one of us kids would claim the spot beneath her. This sounds crazy, but she would lie on her side with her legs bent, and one of us would claim that spot. She formed a sort of pillow. I loved when I got that spot.

This is all I can remember of Mom in my growing-up years. She was a very mixed-up person, unable to cope with life. Who can deal with things when life is falling apart? But Dad tried with all his might to pull it together.

Back at school, I found a spot where I thrived. Our music teacher in the sixth grade had planned a musical with all the sixth-graders, which was one or two classes. This musical included a mistress of ceremonies (MC) and her helper. I was the MC, and I absolutely loved it. I became that person.

I'd had a role in a Halloween play in another school a year or two before—as the head witch. (There were three of us.) The poor teacher! At the last minute, I decided that we three witches could do better, so I jazzed up the lines. Don't ask me what the lines were; I don't remember. But I sure do remember how mad that teacher was. I remember that musical vividly, since I had the starring role. At one point, I lost my program, but I pulled it off with flying colors by blaming my sidekick—and by adlibbing. The poor assistant got the brunt of a lot of things. Afterward, my brother said his classmates asked if I was that mean at home.

How would things have turned out differently for me if this outlet—this talent—had been fostered? It never happened, because my parents had too many things consuming their lives and energy. In the fifth grade, I wanted to take piano lessons, but of course I couldn't. I can't blame them. It's amazing they're even alive with all that was happening.

I found attention in another way. I started developing physically at a very young age. I have a family movie from when I was nine years old, and it was quite evident that I had a bust line and hips even then. My brothers used to call me BB for Big Butt, and it wasn't long before BB applied to another part of my anatomy. Poor Briana, who was four years older, was flat-chested for a long time, and my nickname rubbed salt in her wounds.

2
New Development

I was approaching junior high school, which was in town. The boys were just getting interested in girls at this point, and there I was wearing a C-cup bra at the age of twelve. I had discovered a new way to get attention: my body. It was pretty heady stuff, and I had no one to guide me in it. My mom, love her though I did, was falling apart.

I found myself letting boys "feel me up." But it didn't make me feel good on the inside. I felt dirty, but I also felt I needed the attention. It also felt good physically, which created a vicious cycle.

A man came to our school and talked about the Lord. He was very different from what I had been exposed to in church. He seemed to really care about people. He invited everyone to come to his church and get involved with its youth group. I latched on to that quickly, like a drowning person would a lifeline. Here was some attention that felt good and right to receive, not dirty. But, alas, the other things had been stirred up and were right below the surface, waiting to be let loose.

I got involved with one of the boys at that church. When we were supposed to be in choir practice, we found a place to "practice" other things. We necked. (Mind you, I was still only twelve.) And things were heating up; there was nothing to stop me. I just dug deeper and deeper in.

This churchgoing phase didn't last long—not with the guilt accompanying my double life. I knew deep down inside that I was a hypocrite, so I faded away from church life. It didn't help that I was the only one in the whole family that expressed an interest in church at the time. My dad would drop me off there and pick me up afterward.

I had one friend at that time. Her name was Denise, and she lived down the road from me a bit. I used to spend the night at her house a lot. Her father was a sleazy kind of guy that I made sure not to be around much. He had a tendency to want to touch me, which was pretty yucky. Although I knew my body was a great attention-getter and used it as such, I had certain things I just wouldn't allow to happen.

Once, when Denise and I were on the bus together, an older girl—around sixteen—got on, started bad-mouthing Denise, and made her give up her seat. I went ballistic. All the pent-up rage erupted, and I attacked this poor girl. She didn't know what hit her. She hadn't said or done anything to me; it was, to say the least, a case of being in the wrong place at the wrong time.

That was the summer that we started building our new house at Lake Revere. We had bought a lot there when it first opened up. In fact, we bought the first lot sold. I still remember walking around in a huge mud puddle nearby. It was a manmade lake that ended up covering many miles. We used to go there a lot in the summer and swim—long before we ever built our house. It was our summer recreation.

That summer I was thirteen, and I had a boyfriend. One of the salesmen had moved his family there for the summer. He had four children, and Stephen was my age. They were Italian. His older brother, fifteen, would come and pick me up on his small motorcycle and take me out for the day. I was linked up with Stephen, and several of us started to party big-time. Stephen and I were the youngest at age thirteen. The others were sixteen and eighteen. We would get beer and really tie one on. Meanwhile, my necking went further and further.

We finished our house and moved into it that summer. And I had already set the foundation for quite a summer. It was so wild; yet somehow I was still a virgin. Everything but intercourse had happened, but the completion was fast approaching. And I certainly had a reputation at that point.

Then Stephen and his family moved back to wherever they had come from. Boy, was I at loose ends. At that point, the salesmen started making overtures. I couldn't take it anymore, and I tried to commit suicide for the first time. How? I tried to swim across the lake, hoping to drown. It was my first cry for help. I would've never succeeded, since I was a fairly fit girl.

3
A New Start

So I had a chance to start afresh, to make new friends and start out on a new path. But the patterns had already been set. The sexual angle had set up housekeeping. It was the strong, ruling part of my life. And I felt trapped. I would get involved and immediately allow liberties, since I thought I would be rejected if I didn't. This brought so much attention. Unfortunately, it also set me up for rejection, which made me feel like a used-up piece of trash. Easy girls don't get any respect; they just get dumped. It was a vicious cycle. In my endeavor to be accepted, I was constantly setting myself up for rejection after rejection.

Of course, I was still drinking *big*-time. Then my brother, Peter, turned me on to something new: pot. He had been smoking it for a long time. My first try was so potent, I look back and wonder if it had been laced with something else.

Devin, my boyfriend at the time (who also had an unhappy home life), and I decided we were going to run away. It was a spur-of-the-moment thing. We left school and somehow got in touch with one of his friends. He gave us a ride out of town. We spent our first night in that car in the woods. Devin and I were finally going to get to make love all the way. But we couldn't, because I was too small; little girls just don't do those things at that age.

We kept hitchhiking our way further and further from our town. At one point, some college students picked us up. Things between Devin and I were going sour. (Of course they were! We were only children trapped in children's bodies.) We partied with the college students that night, and Devin and I parted ways. One of the students took me into some woods to spend the night hiding and hopefully get a piece. He couldn't either. I was so fortunate that he didn't insist on it. Looking back, I know God was looking out for me.

The college student left, and that night I came up with a plan. I was going to hitchhike on my own to Roanoke and hook up with some students there. It was horrible waking up the next day. I had slept on the ground with only a sheet, and it was very cold. I woke up sober, only vaguely remembering where I was. I just started walking and ultimately found my way onto a highway.

Some truck drivers picked me up. The first two stopped at a hotel with me that night. They were considering sex, of course, but something held them back. I now know what that something was: fear of statutory rape charges. I was faking sleep and heard them talking about turning me in. They knew I was a lot younger than I said, which was nineteen. The dead giveaway was when I showed them some school pictures of me and my classmates. They certainly looked their and my age of thirteen.

Well, I made it through the night, and at the next

truck stop got a ride from another truck driver. It was a repeat story. Here was some old guy thinking he was going to get a free piece. I was sitting in the truck, waiting for him to come back with some food, when another truck driver came up and told me that some guys were planning a gang rape. Needless to say, I made tracks real fast.

At that point, running away no longer seemed as appealing as it had. I had been gone for thirteen days. I decided to turn myself in. It was the wee hours of the morning, and I was hitchhiking again—this time to the closest police station. A group of rowdy, drunk teenage boys picked me up. This time I was not so lucky. I got drunk with them, and one of the guys started the usual. But he wasn't too big for me. But the experience was sour. The other guys must have been turned off because mercifully there was no gang rape accompanied by violence or worse.

I did finally find my way to the police station, and my parents were notified. The police were very kind to me, and they didn't put me in a jail cell. It had to be pretty evident that I had been through a lot. They gathered up what seemed like a mountain of pillows and found me a warm spot to sleep in until my parents arrived to take me home.

4
The Mental Ward

Needless to say, when I got home, I was a pretty mixed-up cookie. I tried to get back into the swing of things but nothing "fit." I couldn't cope. I found myself longing to die, and I took a *bunch* of aspirin, trying to bring it about. Fortunately, it was not enough to cause any harm. It was just another cry for help.

Because I had been exposed to family members going into mental hospitals, it wasn't a foreign concept to me. I told my parents I wanted just that, so they admitted me to the mental ward of a local teaching hospital. It was quite a trip. I was locked up completely and found myself in the midst of some very sick people. And, of course, I got involved with one of the male patients on the ward.

One of the things that surfaced there was my hatred toward my father. All the years I had spent trying to replace what I felt was the lost love of my father erupted into irrational hatred and anger. I lashed out at him and refused to see him when I was in the hospital. I also told him I hated him. Looking back, I know now that I caused him immense pain. Even as I write this, it hurts.

It was decided that I would benefit from being in a

mental hospital, not just in a ward at a teaching hospital. So I was transferred to a private hospital several hundred miles away. What a place! It had separate wards, floors—whatever you want to call them.

The highest ward was called the open ward. It wasn't terribly different from the regular floor of a hospital, except the rooms were similar to those in a hotel. In this part of the hospital you might get a room to yourself, but more often you'd have a roommate and share a private bath. The patients had many moments of freedom to roam the grounds. They were still locked up, but they could get out on their own at certain times. The grounds were absolutely beautiful. There was even a greenhouse and some therapy there. They also had occupational therapy, such as ceramics and other art.

Then there was the semi-open ward. It was basically the same, but there was no unsupervised grounds-roaming. And there were wards that were far from open or anything vaguely resembling a motel. These were the locked and semi-locked wards where the "real crazies" were kept.

Oh yes, I failed to mention that this hospital had a two-lane bowling alley in the basement, and I must say it was indeed fun.

When I arrived at this place, I was placed in the semi-open ward. Being consistent, I sought out a male companion. Of course, there were no opportunities for romantic interludes that went very far, since contact between the sexes was limited to dining and group settings.

Then I was at it again. One guy smuggled in some

drugs, and we split them. Me being the incredibly naive person that I was, I told my roommate, who reported me to the higher-ups. This brought about a quick change in my status on the semi-open ward.

I bet you were wondering how I knew all this stuff about the other wards. It was from personal experience. I soon discovered what other kinds of accommodations existed in other parts of the hospital. I could even say the bowels of the hospital. The memory is very vivid in my mind. A male nurse escorted me into the very bowels of that hell pit. We traversed *down, down, down,* unlocking jail-like doors as we went. I was placed in the most closed ward in the whole hospital. And I'd thought I was among sick people before. *Whoa!*

Each patient was given a private room—or should I say cell. You had a bed, and your door was heavy steel with a ten-by-twelve-inch window. The lights were never completely out but dimmed, even throughout the night. Carpeting did not exist in this region of the hospital. All shared a large bathroom, and there was an open nurses' station—a glassed-in sort of cage—in the center of the ward. To this day, I don't remember ever using that bathroom, but I must have. I guess I don't want to think about that bathroom, since it was rumored that if someone really messed up, she was submerged in a tub full of ice with only her head poking out of the hole. Yes, I blanked it out.

This ward was a *trip*, and I don't mean a good one. Some of the women were completely out of touch with reality. I remember one woman standing at the window and having conversations with someone that only she was cognizant of. Then there was the girl of eighteen or nineteen who was physically and mentally disabled by drugs; her brain was fried from too many acid (LSD) trips. Some patients on this ward received shock treatments, which seemed to eradicate their memories. Patients came back from shock treatments and were asked to write down everything they could remember. Many of the women could barely fill a single page. This was real and truly scary. *Oh God, I thought, I hope they don't do this to me.*

The only other thing nearly as scary was that ice-filled bathtub thing. I never saw it happen, but the idea sure did make me tremble on the inside. It could have been just a rumor to keep people in line, but I don't think so, in light of all the other horrific things that happened.

My stay had changed drastically. *I was hoping for help and look what I have now,* I thought. It was a whole new world, not anything like I could have imagined. On top of all that, I was still only a child pushing fourteen, I wasn't even sure how old I was at that point, since everything tended to scrunch together.

The hospital had two kinds of doctors: psychiatrists and psychologists. The one pretty much adhered to drug therapy and the other was counseling-oriented. At that time, I was assigned to a psychiatrist who decided to enroll me in drug therapy. I was given strong doses of *Thorazine* and *Stellazine*. The words Thorazine and Stellazine will forever stick in mind as I reflect on my body's initial reaction to those drugs. Talking about being doped up! They were doozies.

The doctor was soon to hear about my feelings

regarding this treatment. I was so angry I wrote him a letter. I can vividly remember not being able to write legibly; the letters grew as I wrote. Did he even receive that letter? I don't know. That drug treatment did nothing to alleviate the emotions pent up within my breast. To the contrary, the anger grew like a fire.

At times we were allowed outside under strict supervision. We would form a small circle and toss the medicine ball—a leather ball of around ten pounds, or maybe more. I had no problem tossing that ball, which surprised some of the male staff who caught it. No, I didn't knock anybody down, but I sure tried.

I stayed on that ward for a while, knowing that when I performed properly, I would again be allowed to go to an open ward. There was some intermingling between our ward and the other semi-locked ward. Sometimes we were allowed contact with the men's ward in a recreational setting, where we'd play Ping-Pong, billiards, etc. Oh the joy! What a trip! There was an assortment of men, women, girls, and boys in this hospital, but the sexes were separated. Any intermingling was closely monitored.

I'm going on a slight sidetrack here to mention shock treatments, which I believe are illegal now, but who knows. You may know someone who experienced them, but you can never visualize the reality of it until you view it firsthand. These people came back in a blacked-out fog. This was therapy? Give me a break.

Well, I did learn to perform pretty darn well. I played the game to get out of that hellhole, and it worked. I was brought back up to the semi-open ward. Was I cured or any better? No way. I had just learned how to bury my anger and burn with rage deep within.

My family made occasional visits, but it was a long time before I would see my father. I cry even now as I reflect on how it was. What hurt and pain I caused him. I can barely begin to imagine. As I look back, I can't say that Dad ever rejected me. But in my small child's mind, I perceived it as such, especially in light of the obvious transfer of his affection to my younger brother. Maybe my father was afraid of his feelings for me and didn't even realize it. But it started something that took a toll on my life, leading me down many paths as I searched for something I felt I had lost.

One thing I know about myself is that I'm an all-or-nothing person. And I had put everything into finding the love I felt I had lost. I went about it with a vengeance, trying anything. During those times, I received some tutoring, but I found myself a good bit behind. Since I was a good student, I was able to catch up upon being released.

Another thing happened when I was at the hospital that I believe made a significant stain. Here it is—that nasty thing I allowed in: One day, when I was gallivanting around on my own in the open ward, I overheard a counseling session and took it totally out of context. The woman said that she could never have an orgasm during lovemaking. The therapist said this was her form of castrating men by never allowing herself this pleasure. Of course, in my sick mind, I latched on to this nasty idea: I'm not worthy of love, so I can't have that pleasure either.

5
Home Again

Well, I had been "cured," and it was time to leave and to try to pick up the pieces of my life again. Of course, the strong medicine accompanied me home. It wasn't long before I quit taking it. The principal at my school was understanding and compassionate. He had even come to visit me when I was initially in the university, before my transfer to the mental hospital. When I started back to school, he told me if I needed to talk at any time, his office was always open to me. He even let me smoke in there if I wanted to. Talk about bending rules!

It was known in the school that I had spent some months in a mental hospital, so I was an outcast and an enigma to my fellow students. A few tried to be friends, but it was just too hard. There was no common denominator. And some patterns were deeply entrenched in my life.

I met a boy my age who had just moved into our private lake community. Tommy was unaware of what had happened to me. He was a friend of my younger brother, and his younger sister of about ten was my friend. Soon I began to hang around with this family. Their father was thirty-four and a very good-looking man. At first I was Tommy's girlfriend, but poor Tommy didn't move fast enough.

Looking back, I can see another dysfunctional family. It was almost like I couldn't feel loved if there was no physical involvement. It also became known that the younger sister was fast, even at her young age. I believe I know the source of this now. Unlike Tommy, Tommy's father was not too slow; he made his interests known. I don't recall how things came about as they did. But it happened when my mother's own path of self-destruction included drinking and sleeping around with men other than my father.

Mom had been messing around a long time, and when we moved, the behavior continued. She had become a secretary out at the lake community. One night, she and I hooked up with two of the salesmen; one of them was Tommy's father. I was still too small for lovemaking, but Mom sure wasn't. She was stone drunk and had no idea what she was doing. Believe me when I tell you that when you mix heavy drinking, you do things you absolutely don't recall at a later time, as I too discovered later in my own life.

Mom accommodated both men, but it didn't end there. On several occasions, she and I would do these things again. And on those occasions, I was always with Tommy's father. Thomas and I would disappear into a motel room for several days at a time, and when we returned to the lake, the guards were on the lookout. But they didn't find us. I should add that Thomas was an alcoholic, and these things were always accompanied by heavy drinking. Could this be why his young daughter was known as a fast girl? Could her father have indoctrinated her into this life? If so, he was a very sick man. But I didn't feel that way or even see it. The many times we were together, we never went "all the way." I was too small, and he was too big. Sick, sick, sick. We even talked about running away and going to Hawaii or on a cruise.

I remember the end of this excursion. We were going back home and had snuck in past the gate when we realized the guard was in hot pursuit. And we escaped discovery one more time.

Thomas and his family soon disappeared from the area. Whatever happened to them? Whatever happened to the wife and mother of those children? I shudder to think about it, and I believe Tommy may have become gay. But who knows?

Well, time passed, and I did make it through what was left of the school year. The summer had arrived.

6
Divorce

It was pretty obvious that my parents' marriage was down the drain, and divorce was imminent. Meanwhile, other things were going on among the other members of my family.

My sister, Briana, had been seeing a guy since we had moved to the lake, and they decided to get married. My father performed the ceremony in our home, which was not attended by his disapproving family members. Briana was very in love with this guy, but he was extremely jealous and possessive to the degree of being neurotic. He didn't even want her to leave the apartment by herself to get the mail. And on top of that, he was physically abusive. They had been married only about six weeks when she got out of the marriage. Fortunately she had a decent job.

The oldest of my siblings escaped and joined the navy. Peter was doing his own thing, sleeping around and partying. Douglas was Douglas and still very close to Dad.

When the divorce happened, Douglas decided to continue living with Dad, and Peter and I moved into an apartment with Mom. I'd say we were living with Mom, but that it isn't the actual truth. The complex where we lived had an adjoining complex. In this adjoining complex, Mom moved in with her current salesman boyfriend, where they lived in an almost continuous state of drunkenness when not working. Peter and I were free to do whatever we wanted. Which was to party like crazy—and party we did. We hooked up with a group of hippies that summer, and we did nothing but party, party, party. You name it; we did it. I slept around a lot, and no longer was I as small as I had been. It was the ultimate hippie experience.

Needless to say, these people were a great deal older than me—late teens and early twenties to my fourteen. I did a whole lot more than pot and drinking. I tried acid, downers, and uppers, but mostly I stuck to drinking and smoking dope.

Well, the summer was over, and so was the party. I found myself in a new school and a year behind. I had missed too much to pass the eighth grade. There I was again among your average fourteen-year-olds. But I was far beyond them. I had experienced so many things in the last year or two that I was really and truly a misfit at that point. The people I had partied with had no room for a little eighth-grader. What a mess! My mother was overwhelmed and couldn't deal with me either, so she had me committed to a mental hospital again.

7
The Mental Hospital Again

Once I resolved myself to being in the hospital again, I found I had to get over the resentment of having Mom commit me. I decided I did want help, and I opened completely up to my psychologist. This time the emphasis was more on counseling. I still had a psychiatrist, but there was no drug therapy or being in that nasty pit I had experienced before.

I was very cooperative. I had group therapy five days a week with my psychologist, in addition to two private sessions a week. The group therapy patients were an assorted gathering of people of different ages and from different backgrounds. As things moved along, I continued to open up. This time I wanted out of the rut, the hell, the vicious cycle, the prison my life had become. So I poured out my heart.

Things moved along. My psychologist encouraged me and tried to build my self-esteem. But that wasn't enough. He was making progress as I tried to accept myself as a girl. I soon found myself wanting to be more feminine and being comfortable with it. My mother had bought me a pretty outfit, and I couldn't wait to wear it. It was a two-piece one with a white, flowing skirt and a matching top that tied under the bust. It was a bit risqué with a good bit of cleavage showing, but I felt marvelous in it.

I attended a group therapy in it one day, and my psychologist expressed how proud he was of me. I can almost hear his words. During most of the sessions, I didn't share out loud, but he knew everything about me from our private sessions. He told the group to stop belly-aching (of course, not in those words, but the implications were clear), and he pointed me out, saying I had been through more than they could ever imagine.

There must be something in me that, once I open up completely to a person, it awakens a desire in that person to protect me. I believe part of it is the naivety of a child, the little girl who was hurt so long ago and still wants love and wants to believe the best of everybody. She thinks this person will love her, and she keeps on trying and always hoping, no matter how much she's rejected.

I see now that my counselor was very unprofessional; he got emotionally involved with me. It never went any further than that. I often wonder where he is now and how his life has progressed. Is he even still alive?

That hospital stay was much shorter than the first. I was released and sent home on an outpatient basis. It just so happened there was a private mental hospital in town where I started my "wonderful" new treatments. Almost immediately afterward, I was readmitted. It seemed I just couldn't get away from those places. One time I added up the time I had spent in various mental hospitals and wards, and it came to fourteen months.

There's something I need to add. During some of my hospital stays, I had a deep fascination with the occult—anything to do with witchcraft, for example. I made numerous jagged drawings, and in my mind they were satanically inspired—just another interesting thing to add to the mix. At this new hospital, my roommate also had some involvement with the occult. The professionals will tell you she had a split personality. This may be true, but I believe there was more involved. There were demons inside this woman. She would be overtaken by them and exhibit totally different people. Once when I saw those personalities take over, I told them to leave in the name of Jesus, and they did; she became lucid as herself. She and I messed around with a Ouija board, and she said she had a friend who was a white witch. Thank God that He had mercy on me and those demons did not attack me.

I decided I wanted nothing else to do with the occult; it was just too scary. I gathered up all of the twenty to thirty drawings and burned every single one. This caused deep pain, but the occult no longer fascinated me.

While in that hospital, I made some progress in trying to accept and love myself—not much, but a little. I was still Miss Fix It. I still believed that if I could fix my family's problems, we would be a normal family and live happily ever after. Or if I could fix somebody's problems, they would accept and love me. Sad, so sad.

It gets better. One day in the hospital, we were all gathered for "community time," when all the patients congregated informally. It was a small hospital, so the gathering was like a club meeting. A friend of mine, who had a cast on, brought up a grievance against another friend of mine. They were at it tooth and nail, and it was getting heated. I was trying to protect my friend from the other and got smack-dab in the middle.

He was very angry, and she was lying there with a broken leg. He just lost it and threw scalding hot coffee at her. But guess who received the contents. Miss Fix It. Yes, I got some pretty bad burns on my face; the coffee scorched off a layer or two in places. They took me to the local hospital and gave me a shot of codeine. I was sent back to the other mental hospital, and miracle of all miracles, my face healed very quickly with no scarring.

8
On The Road Again

My stay in this hospital ended abruptly and tragically one day. I say tragically because things had been set in motion for me to attend a Baptist boarding school. It was just a matter of time before I would go there. But, alas, one night I got mad and decided to run away. I slipped out of one of the windows, which were supposedly made in such a way as to make it impossible to get out. But where there's a will, there's a way.

I just took off, got on the highway, and started trucking to other places with my thumb sticking out. *Hey,* I reasoned, *I'll go far away down South and make it on my own.* I didn't have any plans on how this was to come about, but I was determined it would happen.

My first ride was with a truck driver. (At least I was consistent.) We made a stop before leaving town—in a bedroom, of course. Old habits die hard. I was trapped into thinking this was my only way to get things done. I just couldn't say no. This guy supplied me with a few Black Beauties—a very potent form of speed—and he was the only guy on that trip that included sex. I was flying pretty high, going from one state to the next. The next truck driver was not so demanding.

I made it all the way to Alabama before I lost heart and decided to turn myself in. There I was given my first taste of juvenile hall, and it was a very bitter pill indeed. I didn't fit in there either. Even the girls there detected something alien about me. It didn't help that I was coming off some pretty strong speed. I ended up in isolation. I just couldn't deal with that at all.

My dad showed up to get me, and we started traveling back to our home state. He chose not to put me back in the hospital, and the boarding school wouldn't take me since I had run away from the hospital. My father had no choice but to let me live with him. I was fifteen years old.

9
Home Again

I started high school while living with Dad. I was now in the ninth grade—oh joy. I tried to fit in. Almost immediately, I got back together with my old friends, the ones I'd partied with the summer I lived with Mom. I went back to one of my heretofore-unmentioned old ways: petty shoplifting.

During all those years from the age of thirteen on, I had been on birth control pills. Sad, isn't it, that parents put their children on these things. My parents knew I was promiscuous, and they at least had the "sense" to keep me supplied with some form of birth control so as not to bring unwanted babies into this world. This is one reason I never had to deal with an abortion or a teenage pregnancy during all those wild years. Somehow I always made sure I took the pill. This did not keep me from picking up gonorrhea from time to time. But thank God it was treatable and went away—unlike herpes. And only by the grace of God was AIDS not a prevalent disease at that time, or I would not be here writing this many years later.

I went to school sporadically. My weekends were spent with my old pals. It may seem strange, but I had found a group I could fit in with and hang out with. I called them my "boys." I was one of the boys. They could always count on me for a good time. There was no respect, but I was one of them.

One special guy came to our town on weekends, and he'd look me up. He was probably the only one I ever came close to being in love with, but there were no strings attached on either side. Sometimes when I hooked up with this guy, pictures were taken of me in lace-up boots doing the you-know-what. Of course, those pictures were spread around. Oh joy, a record of my misdeeds.

Most of the time my promiscuous behavior was accompanied by drunkenness. The old saying about drinking being a demon is aptly put. I would get completely out of control when I drank. There are sections of my life I don't recall—and other parts I will never reveal. My wild living had become a driving force in my life. I was trapped. The wilder I lived, the worse it got. I had to keep drinking to forget what I had done the night before or the weekend before.

I can't say every weekend was spent with the boys. There was ample opportunity to find other weekend amusements in that university town in the mid-seventies. It had a reputation across the country for being one of the biggest partying universities around. If you were a free-and-easy girl, there was a lot of free partying. Often I would go to fraternity parties, where the beer ran freely and in large quantities—not to mention a few local bars right around the university, where you could also get easily picked up. I often did.

But even those bars drew the line at too much wildness. One night I went too far, even for this partying crowd, and the manager had me physically thrown out. I had worn out my welcome. If other managers had taken strong measures like that one, could things have been different?

Then there was the night I went to a party across town. I got stone drunk and was tripping on a little acid when I met up with the boy I ran away with the first time. He and I hooked up for a few days, but he couldn't deal with the fact that I was so loose. I left one of those parties on that side of town, and for once I was by myself. I woke up in the ice room of a Holiday Inn. You know the place; each floor has a central ice machine where guests go and help themselves. It one was enclosed and *warm*. It was a safe place to sleep it off. One of the guests contacted the management, and I was asked to leave. I could've been thrown in jail. If I had been a guy, I probably would have.

Changing gears again. I had hooked up with the boys at a party. And I guess I just walked off. It was winter in Virginia, and I didn't even have my shoes on. At least I had my clothes on. A taxi driver took pity on me and drove me to my dad's at no charge. Stumbling up to the door, I tripped on a piece of cinder block and gouged my shin so badly I still carry the scar to this day.

During one of my other excursions, I got hooked up with some people I didn't know much about. It's funny that I would actually have standards about who I slept with. If I didn't like the way he looked, forget it. Well, there was a bunch of us in a van. I had known one of the girls growing up. Well, this was one of those times I didn't like the guy they hooked me up with, which did not make him too happy. He started to rough me up, I guess. I don't really know except for the bruises the next day. They dumped me in the country, and I woke up in somebody's barn with no idea where I was.

I decided to walk down the road to the nearest house to ask if I could use the phone and call my dad to pick me up. I remember those people so well. They were a warm and loving family, and they graciously allowed me into their home and let me sleep on a small bed in the laundry room. They were Christians—that much I know. I'm not sure how, but I know.

Poor Dad was so embarrassed and angry when he picked me up. I have no idea how he dealt with all that I was doing. Every weekend I was gone, and if he questioned me, I cussed him out and told him it was none of his business. I had become a ward of the state and supposedly was on probation. My father had gone to court asking them to do this. But my probation officer had no idea of my behavior. I guess Dad couldn't bring himself to turn me in—until the day things caught up with me, and it took care of itself.

10
Locked Up

I had gone into a 7-Eleven store. Following my usual practice, I was shoplifting and grabbed a bag of Funyuns. I guess the manager was fed up. He called the police, and oh, were they happy to see me. They took me in. Unfortunately, the policeman who took me in had had experiences with my family through Douglas, who had been very busy in his escapades.

No, I was not the only wild member in this family. Peter and I would often cross paths in our partying. And he knew of my reputation. It was a well-known fact in town, actually. He didn't pass too much judgment; but Douglas didn't want anything to do with me. He would rather have been disassociated from me altogether. He was ashamed, and who could blame him. He had many run-ins with the law but somehow always seemed to elude them.

So this particular policeman had it in for our family. I had never encountered him, but Douglas had gotten the upper hand on him. I don't know how, but he had.

So the irony was that I would have my own encounter with this police officer, who had a reputation of his own of being mean and nasty, especially to juveniles. Guess who got the brunt of this. On the way upstairs to the cell they placed me in, the policeman roughed me up.

They contacted my father, who had just had too much. He refused to pick me up, and since I had broken probation, I was docketed to go to juvenile court. So Juvenile Hall, here I come. Guess who had the pleasure of transporting me there? Mr. Geniality himself. It has to be one of the worst experiences I've ever had. There was a policeman up front driving, and I was handcuffed in the backseat with this man for a drive an hour away. He tormented me verbally the whole way, telling I was nothing but trash eaten up with VD. I never said a word to him, but I burned with hatred and anger.

I stayed there for a few weeks, with my sixteenth birthday fast approaching. There was one beautiful ray of light there: a man visiting as a volunteer from one of the local churches nearby. He shared about the Lord with any of us who were interested. He gave a Bible to any who desired one. I started praying and thinking about Jesus again. There was a rekindled interest.

Soon I had to go back to court. It was decided that I'd go to the Diagnostic Center for diagnosis, which would determine where I'd be placed. Most of the youth who went to the Diagnostic Center were placed in reform schools and went through the program in as few as three to six months. They were then sent home, or to a halfway house and then home.

In light of my history with mental hospitals, I was to be sent to a residential treatment center in another state. Until all the red tape could be unraveled, I would spend time in the reform school. Oh joy. The wait was six months, the same amount of time it would have taken for me to go through the treatment program.

But while I was waiting in the Diagnostic Center, I started praying and reading my Bible daily. It looked like there was hope in sight. I did lose sight of this as time dragged on in the reform school, but I was back in school every day, learning, learning, learning all the subjects we need to get along. And yes, I conformed to the system there.

11
The Residential Treatment Center

I would be slightly remiss if I didn't mention how I got to the treatment center. A woman met me at the reform school, and we loaded all my many things to go to the airport and fly out of Virginia to the lovely state of Mississippi so far away. Hah hah. They hadn't done their homework very well. It just so happened I was far from Virginia, but I was close to another huge party place: New Orleans. Talk about ironies.

The treatment center resembled a campus. But there the resemblance ended. It contained kids who had been rejected by every other place. Nobody wanted them. And it often seemed that the adult staff fit in that description too. But one woman was completely different.

She stood out in her compassion and caring for the kids there. She made no bones about her Christianity, but she was not offensive. She was very gentle, loving, accepting, and just so sweet. Many were drawn to her because of these qualities—me included. She would take anybody who wanted to go to church with her, and I started going. It was my first exposure to a full-gospel church. And it was my first experience with seeing the gifts of the Holy Spirit in practice. When someone gave a prophecy in tongues, it fascinated me. When I returned to the center, I told one of the staff members about how different these people seemed. I said their eyes shined. He said, "I've seen that when people are in love." Then he just shrugged it off as something not real. But that's those people in love with someone—with Jesus. Well, I wanted to embrace it, and I tried. But I didn't have any staying power.

Finally I had the okay to make a weekend visit home. But that home was in the aforementioned story about the boys and wandering off in a drunken stupor to end up home and with a scar. *So much for Christianity,* I thought. *I just can't do it.* I went back to the treatment center cold inside. I didn't care anymore. I found myself a boyfriend and got used and dumped again. I couldn't care less.

There was a hierarchy in the center. Four of the girls *ruled.* For the most part, I steered clear of them. But when I was away, they decided to steal some of my stuff. Knowing the state of mind I was in upon returning, it was the wrong thing to do. I wanted to get my stuff back, and they denied taking it. They came to my room later that night to show me who was boss. They began to taunt me just like that police officer had. I just clammed up and closed them out; I didn't respond at all. At least not on the outside. On the inside I was burning with rage.

For hours, these girls tried everything to get a response from me. Then one them blew it: she sat on my bed and touched my breast. The volcano *erupted.* The ringleader had challenged me, and I had told her I would fight her. But they only worked as a team. I tore into them like a vicious animal. They couldn't stop me. One girl lost a tooth. One tried to get the other girls to quit and tried to stop me as they were losing. She had me under the arms but this still didn't stop me. I used my feet to kick out.

It finally took one of the counselors, who weighed around two hundred pounds, sitting on me to get me to stop. They put me in isolation that night, saying it was for my own protection. Was it for my protection or theirs?

12
On The Road Again

I made my plans. I was going to hitchhike to New Orleans and go to a runaway center that someone at the treatment center had told me about. And that's what I proceeded to do.

It wasn't that hard to leave the center. We were locked up only at night. The first ride I got was with an elderly Christian man. He bought me something to eat. My next ride was with a young guy. He took me to his apartment. He was a newlywed and showed me his wedding pictures, and he had the audacity to think I was going to bed with him. I couldn't believe it. He had been married such a short time. I disillusioned him pretty quickly.

I made it to the runaway center, but they said they had to contact someone about me. I called my grandparents, and they decided they would try to give me a home. I stayed with them a few months. I had my bedroom in the back of the house and cooked for myself out in the garage, which had a stove and a refrigerator. I stocked up my refrigerator with beer and couldn't understand why they were so mad at me for drinking out there. I got a job at the local Burger King, working the three-to-eleven shift. I closed every night and got home late.

Finally my grandparents had had enough and told me I had to leave. I found my own apartment and was living on my own at sixteen, almost seventeen. How, you might ask, did I get this place? Simple. I lied and used my sister's Social Security number. And believe me, she has never let me forget it. I was working at a local doughnut shop.

Of course, I was still sexually active. But it wasn't the same. When I was home, I had been "one of the boys"; it wasn't like that down there. It was just a constant series of rejections. One of the guys I hooked up with told me about massage parlors in the French Quarter. He introduced me to the people who ran them. Now, these were actually legitimate at the time; it was a big-time tourist trap. Men would come in for a massage, thinking they were going to get something more—especially in light of the extras that the girls offered and the line "If you give me a nice tip, I'll make it worth your while." There was an extra labeled "Tulips Delight," which in all reality was nothing more than window cleaner.

Every area of a man's body was touched or massaged except for one. I'll let you figure out which one. When everything was over, you said, "That's all, folks," and directed them to the shower. Major rip-off. But we did give them a good all-over, thirty-minute massage for the basic twenty-five dollars. Extras cost more.

What some of the girls did after hours was their business, and I'm sure there was plenty. Fortunately, I worked the eight-to-four shift at the parlor and saw very little traffic. And on most occasions, I worked alone. Tell me God wasn't looking out for me even then. My partying took on the same patterns. Most of it consisted of heavy drinking accompanied by a little weed now and then.

While working in the parlor, I met Sapphire. We became pretty good friends, although her roommate, Belinda, hated my guts. She and Belinda had been rooming together for a couple of years and through several states. I don't believe they were gay, but Belinda was very possessive. Several times when I was drunk, Sapphire would haul me off to where they were staying, and I would sleep it off.

One time I went to a rock concert with some people from work but got separated while going back and forth to get beer. I got sloshed, and it was time to go home. I didn't know where I was and got picked up by two guys. We did the rounds and partied till the wee hours. This was one of those times when I got a flea in my ear and decided I didn't want to put out. We were hours away from New Orleans, and this guy just couldn't believe I had led him on all night. I lost my glasses, which happens to be a big deal when you're half blind without them.

They abandoned me at some Stop-N-Go store. I guess they figured since I wouldn't put out, they would put me out. Thank God they didn't rape me or leave me as roadkill. I came out of the store, and they were gone, gone, gone. Some guy had seen all this happen and offered to help me out. He took me to a room. He didn't expect anything in return. But of course I felt I had to pay my way, and I knew of only one way to do that. He bought me a bus ticket the next day and sent me back to New Orleans. He even tried to look me up a few weeks later, but it was a no-go for me.

13
Booking it Again

I hooked up with one of the guys around the parlor. We hit it off. We were going to go to Boston and start a rock group. Another guy there said he had a rich girlfriend who would put us up and get us started. Well, not very far down the road, our beat-up car broke down. This happened to be in Alabama. We split up, with plans to reunite in Boston.

Neil and I started hitchhiking. We made it by the skin of our teeth, with many close calls at that. Two truck drivers picked us up, and we were going back to a motel room, where we'd party with the booze they had bought. While we were taking turns showering, one of the truck drivers told us we'd better book it. He said his "buddy" had a gun and plans we wouldn't like. While his buddy was in the shower, we made tracks.

When we got to Boston, we never did find the other two guys. Maybe they weren't as "lucky" as we had been. My road down Perversion Alley was getting worse and worse. We ended up hooking up with some gay men. One of them had his own boarding house. He told us if we made love in front him, we could stay in one of the rooms. We were the only straight ones there. But we looked at it as a temporary thing.

One time in our room we had a copy of a book called *The Other*. It was a fiction story about the antichrist. We read it, and it sure did stir up some interesting thoughts. We even started reading in the book of Revelation. I didn't stay with Neil long. I left with two gay hustlers to go who knows where. We hitchhiked to New York City. I still remember my first night there. What a sorry trio we made. Our first night was spent in Central Park on one of the huge boulders. It felt just wonderful. We were not a group that anyone felt compelled to mug. Just the opposite.

We started panhandling, and the guys were discussing how they would go about mugging someone and snatching a purse. Down the sidewalk traipsed Anthony, an obvious homosexual. One of us asked for a cigarette, the other a dime, and I just kind of stood there. He invited us up to his room. He was a hairdresser next door to a Greek restaurant. He mentioned he would introduce me to Carlos, who ran the restaurant along with his business partner, to see if I could work as a waitress there.

My interview, which took place in the office, ended up being a horizontal one. (I am nothing if not consistent.) I started working there and moved in with Carlos and his current girlfriend, who had been hooking on the streets. She wasn't current for long. At that point I had very few qualms about anything. The conscience becomes seared after a while of living on the streets and trying to survive.

I was Carlos's girl. We had an interesting relationship.

He shared an apartment with Arnold, who also worked in the restaurant. Every so many months, they traded hours. One worked twelve hours, then the other worked twelve hours—one worked night hours and the other worked the days. My hours lined up with Carlos's, except I put in only ten hours and had days off once or twice a week. It didn't bother Carlos at all that I shared a bed with Arnold on occasion. Carlos would have been happy if I turned a few tricks even.

One guy who frequented the restaurant was a pimp named Seth, and he was not your usual pimp. He looked like a cowboy in his forties or fifties. The idea of me turning tricks did not appeal to me initially. But the money started to play on my mind. I had been with Carlos for about a month when I decided to investigate this "thing" with Seth.

He took me to an apartment that one of his girls lived in. Slow witted is how she appeared. He proceeded to show me a photo album with all the girls he had working over the past fifteen or twenty years. One man was featured in most of the pictures. It was a younger, much-more-attractive Seth. All of the pictures were explicit.

Then he showed me "the books"—a record of all the johns that this girl serviced. I was thinking, I have to keep records?! Then I asked him about drinking and smoking a little weed while tricking. He said, "It's best if you don't."

I gulped, wondering how I could ever do any of that if I wasn't stoned or smashed. But I didn't close the door. He told me that he knew the man who owned the Font Salad Company and would set up a job for us. This man just liked to watch, and my first job would be doing it with Seth in front of him. I told Seth I'd do it, and we had it set up for the next week.

When I made that decision, something happened on the inside. I froze up completely. Where I had been warm and open with Carlos, I became cold, frigid, and resentful. Inside I blamed him. No longer was I the girl searching for acceptance and love; I had hardened. I quit the waitressing job in light of my upcoming "career move."

During the last few weeks before I decided to change "careers," I had received a tract from someone on the street. This stands out in my memory big-time. It said, "Does your life resemble the dark, dirty, smelly subways in New York?" It proceeded to outline the way out of this smelly place by accepting Jesus.

Then the day came. I went into town with Carlos. We commuted daily from New Jersey. I was to meet Seth and go for my first trick. But he wasn't there and never showed up that whole day. (Don't tell me I don't serve a sovereign God!) I went home with Carlos that night with a huge sigh of relief. I was off the hook. That was it. No career move for me.

I started thinking along the lines of moving out, finding a small, simple job, and going back to church again. Of course it wasn't realistic, but I didn't think about that. I decided to call my father and let him know I was alive. It had been several months since I had left New Orleans, and no one in my family knew where I was. I found out later that my grandmother had gone to the morgue to make sure I wasn't there.

Rachel Rosebud

When I got my dad on the phone, he was overjoyed to hear from me. I asked if I had gotten any mail. Before I left New Orleans, Sapphire and Belinda had left before me, and I had given Sapphire my home address. She had sent a letter there, and Dad read it to me on the phone. She wrote about how she had ended up in Arkansas; she and Belinda lived there in exchange for working on the ranch. She had asked Christ to come into her life and had been praying for me fervently the last month.

That was all it took. I told Dad I had to hang up and I would call back later. I was on my knees calling out to God with all my heart, asking for forgiveness and inviting Him back into my life. I had had enough.

What joy indescribable! What peace! What a relief! I had been so bent over and overwhelmed with sin, but I was free. What a miracle!

PART 2

14
New Life

This new change was for real. I told Carlos I could no longer sleep with him, since we weren't married. He said, "Okay, we'll get married."

I was reading my Bible every day, and things were so different. It was as though a veil had been removed from my eyes. At one point, Carlos brought home a girl who was bisexual because I had told him I always wanted a three-way. Fortunately, I didn't find her appealing, because maybe the temptation would have been too much at that early stage in my new life. It was the last temptation of that sort.

Something else very significant occurred. I had been consumed by alcohol. Not a day passed that I didn't drink some, and many days I drank myself into oblivion. I smoked weed, but it didn't have the hold over me that drink did. When I asked Christ into my life, He took away all desire to drink. I had no period of dry heaves or going to AA or anything along those lines. I know there are people who benefit from these programs and have to work through the process of putting things and issues behind them. But, in my case, the Lord stepped in and miraculously delivered me. I didn't even consider it at the time; it was just *gone*.

A few days passed, and it seemed that Carlos truly loved me and wanted me to be his wife. But it didn't sit right with me. I decided I would call Sapphire out in Arkansas and see if they needed more help on the ranch. When I called, she was overjoyed to hear from me. She said she had been praying for me over the last month. Could some of those prayers have been what kept me alive? I sure think so.

I told her how I had asked the Lord to come into my life and proceeded with my question. Sight unseen, she said, "Yes, come on out." I would have hitchhiked across the country from New York to Arkansas, but Arnold suggested I ask Carlos and some of his brothers for some money to fly. It was a much better way to travel.

The memory is sharp in my mind of arriving in that new place. Sapphire was at the airport with Maryellen and Ralph to pick me up. We proceeded to eat out at Denny's. My language still needed cleaning up; it was as foul as a sailor's. But after dinner and sensing Maryellen's reaction to my mouth, I quit. As simple as that. She never said a word, but it was pretty clear.

Life there was a great change. The location was awesome. We were nestled in the Ozark Mountains, very close to the Oklahoma line. It was breathtaking. Ten of us were residing there at the time. There was a main lodge with a kitchen and dining facilities; a house for Maryellen, Ralph, and their two sons, aged twelve and thirteen; and several cabins placed throughout. The owners of the lodge had let Maryellen and Ralph stay there free. It was a ministry. Ralph was a pastor and part-time ranch hand to the local ranchers. In addition, newlyweds Paula and Ben were living in one of the cabins. Sapphire and Belinda were in another cabin, and I moved in with them.

Often we would open one of the other cabins to people in need passing through. Ralph would come home with some of the most unusual people. One time he picked up a whole family out hitchhiking; they even had a baby with them. They stayed overnight, got a good meal, cleaned up, and went on their way.

Those who wanted to stay long had to work for their keep. I was one of them, as my stay was about five months. Initially, I worked at anything that was necessary, such as cleaning cabins, helping with meals, and cleaning up after dinner. I was just thrilled to be in a place where there was a family. Maryellen and Ralph became my surrogate parents. It was as though I was given the opportunity to go back to when all the crazy stuff had started—back to age thirteen—and to have the chance to grow up again in a normal setting. These people became my family—the family I never had. It was a fresh beginning.

Of course, there were flies in the ointment. Although Sapphire and Belinda had both had an experience with the Lord, I still got bad vibes from Belinda. She was the one who was Sapphire's roommate and had hated me in New Orleans. I guess she had thought she was rid of me when they left town. Such is life; some things are not meant to be.

I still wanted people to like me and tried very hard—too hard. One day, I told Ralph about this, and he taught me a valuable lesson I'll never forget. He said, "Chelsea, you need to let Jesus be the bridge between you and others and not worry about what they think of you." This has stayed with me all these years.

But some habits take a long time to die. One day, shortly after arriving at God's Ranch, I buttonholed Sapphire. She had written to me about the baptism of the Holy Spirit, an experience that intrigued me. I had been exposed to it at the residential treatment center when I went to church with one of the staff members. We were down in our cabin, and I eagerly questioned her about tongues. I wanted it too. She just laughed at me and said, "You don't ask for tongues, stupid. You ask for the baptism of the Holy Spirit." We proceeded to pray, and I asked for the baptism of the Holy Spirit. Whoa! The difference was like night and day. It was like I had been looking at the world through a filter. Things were brighter and clearer. I was so excited. I wanted all I could get my hands on.

One night when Sapphire was working, I was alone in our cabin. She and Belinda had found night jobs in a town about thirty minutes away. Many of the nights I spent alone and was dead to the world when they arrived home after work. This night, there was something outside my door.

By that time in my life, I had exposed myself to many spiritually dark things. Here goes a little doctrine or whatever you want to call it: Many Christians will tell you that a Christian can't have a demon within; the Holy Spirit can't reside with dark spirits in the same vessel. Others will tell you this isn't true. I know that we are all subject to many things; the Bible does talk about spiritual warfare. If it didn't exist, why would it be mentioned? Others say we can be buffeted. In other words, it's an external thing. Well, guess what. The result is the same—inside or outside. If you give it a place, it can wreak havoc in your life.

Anyway, going back to that night: I had gone to sleep only to be awakened shortly afterward by a scratching sound at the door. It could have been a wild animal, but I was scared to death. It seemed there were demons outside my door that were furious at being booted out of my life and wanting back in. Needless to say, I didn't open the door but spent a considerable amount of time praying in my heavenly language. The noises ceased.

I decided to look for a job. There was a small restaurant a few miles down the road. I started waitressing again there. Maryellen, Ralph, Ben, or whoever would take me to work and pick me up after my shift. I enjoyed the work, but my boss seemed overworked. She did all the cooking, and her husband sat around all day drinking beer and occasionally washing dishes. She made the best homemade pies, and at the end of the week, she would send me home with all the extra pieces.

I met a forest ranger one day who seemed to take an interest in me. He was well into his twenties, maybe even pushing thirty. He called me and visited me at the lodge one night. Maryellen and Ralph would not forbid me to date, but they were very concerned. During his visit, a mouse darted out, and he flipped. I never heard from him again.

The job ended abruptly one day when my boss chewed

me out big-time. I quit on the spot. I was so sensitive, I just lost it. I was in tears when I asked Ralph to pick me up. After I told him what happened, he waited a few days and made me go back and apologize. I did look for other work, but nothing was available.

Then something new happened. A new guy, Jake, had moved into the area, and we had started a small Bible study in the town a few miles away. Sapphire, Belinda, and I went to a young married couple's home once a week for the study. Jake had started working with the married guy. What a hunk! He was six four with blond hair and blue eyes, half German and half Swedish. Belinda had him earmarked for Sapphire, but I had the first opportunity to meet him. This just added fuel to the fire where Belinda and I were concerned.

We started dating. He was twenty-five, and I was seventeen. I thought I was in love, but it was just a case of infatuation. I had been thinking about going back to Virginia. My dad was going to help me go back to school, and I was thinking of becoming a nurse. One night when Jake took me home, he asked me if he could send me to nursing school. I said, "How?"

He said, "Why don't you stay here and marry me, and then I'll send you to school?"

Of course I wanted to marry this guy. But another part of me knew I had to go back home and try to mend all the broken pieces. There was so much hurt I had caused, especially to my father. He had been so happy to hear about me coming to the Lord, and I knew I just had to go back.

I told Jake this, and he said he'd wait for me. So I

planned on going back home, attending school, and then going back out to marry Jake. After I returned home, I wrote to Maryellen and often referred to my future wedding. Then one day she called and told me the truth. After I left, Jake had started dating other young girls almost immediately.

What a crushing experience! But I had seen many of the signs beforehand that it wouldn't have worked. Even in my Christian infancy, I was stronger spiritually than he was, and he had been a Christian for years. He had certainly lost his zeal for the Lord.

15
New Beginnings at Home

When I first went home, Dad and Douglas were living in his two-bedroom house. I slept in the living room on a pullout sofa. This was all so new to me.

Dad had vowed never to darken the door of a church again unless one of his children initiated it. When he went through his divorce, the church had turned their back on him and given him no support whatsoever. He had gone to a Spirit-filled charismatic church when I mysteriously disappeared. I don't know what led him there. He asked them to pray for me. It was the kind of church I wanted to attend, so we started going together. My good old Baptist daddy and I went there faithfully. He never entered into the worship but always went with me.

There were other tangible changes at home. Dad had been active in PWP, Parents Without Partners, for quite some time and dated regularly. Sometimes I would go with him to the meetings. He shared with me about one of the women in the group who had cancer. I just did what was natural; I said, "Dad, can we pray for her?" It was just the two of us in the house at that moment, so we sat down at the dining room table, and I began to pray. Dad couldn't stay in the room; he was in tears and went to his room. It was just too much for him. God was restoring a completely broken relationship between a father and a daughter. He is the healer of all things.

Then there was the time that will always be one of the special blessings in my life. One day when I had been home for a while, I went to Douglas's room and knocked on his door. "Who is it?" he said.

I opened the door, stood in the doorway, and said, "Guess what."

"What?"

I replied, "I love you," and closed the door and left.

I had never said that to him. Here the sister he had wanted to disown had come back home a changed person, and it was for real.

One day, some time later, I heard a bunch of carrying on, banging, and clanging. At the time we had an unfinished attic. It had potential, but it was unheated and uncooled. We used to go up there to smoke weed. Well, I soon discovered what all the clatter was about: Douglas had moved all his stuff into the attic and was giving me his room. He couldn't say "I love you," but what better way to show his love. I sure did appreciate my own room.

One day, about a month later, when I was in my newly acquired bedroom, I heard a knock at my door. I said, "Who is it?"

The reply came as the door opened. Douglas said "Guess what."

"What?"

"I love you." And he gently closed the door and left.

What a sweet God I serve to give me something I had never had in my family. I can't say it was restoration, because it had never existed between my brother and me before.

It wasn't long before other family members decided to come back home and live with Dad. The next was Peter. He moved into the living room to the sofa bed I had recently vacated. This wasn't too much of a problem, as he is so easygoing. But along with him came all his partying ways. He hadn't given up that lifestyle, nor had Douglas. Then Briana came home also. This led to some arguments, since she is not so easy to get along with. She moved in to my tiny room with me.

What a household! Everything was dumped on Dad again.

Some of my old friends who were friends with Peter would stop by. They would go to my room to smoke weed, since it was somewhat private. I had been feeling lonely and had not made any new friends at the church yet. My two brothers, my sister, and a married couple I had known before were over. Peter had a bong, which had two bowls filled with a more potent type of weed. I was in the room but not partaking. I just wanted to be around because they were my friends.

As they proceeded to get stoned, they passed the bong around. Peter had just reloaded the bowls. I looked at him and said, "Pass it to me." He handed me the bong, but not before a stunned, pregnant silence fell upon the room. I was on the threshold of a very important decision. I said, "Peter, light me up."

He said, "I'm not going to. If you do it, you'll have to

light it yourself." It was as if everyone in that room was holding their breath.

I couldn't do it. I got up and left the room.

It was evident to all those people that there had been a great change in my life. They wouldn't actually come out and talk about or even acknowledge it, but it was important to them to see my changed life. Here was someone who was completely different. I just wished they could also experience and lay hold of what I had, which was a relationship in the heavenly realms with Jesus. It is simple, but God does not force us. We have to invite Him into our life. Sad to say that many people miss out in this area, since there is the *only way*, and it is through Jesus Christ alone.

16
Working

During those months at home, I looked for a job. I had jobs in several places, one of which was making sandwiches. I also wanted to move away from the crowded living and away from the temptations at home. So I did. I moved into an unfinished basement to share a room with a woman I met at church. We had a bedroom and a bathroom.

At the beginning of that summer, I worked with this woman at a summer camp for retarded children. There was a chunk of time between checks, and we lived off bread and peanut butter. The church we attended had some weird survival biscuits that were kind of like graham crackers, coming from who knows where, and we ate them for breakfast. Dad would have fed me, but I was so darned proud I wouldn't tell him I was practically starving. No, I wasn't anorexic. Believe me, I would've eaten given the chance.

Another job I held was at the Howard Johnson's restaurant before I moved from Dad's. Pride got in my way there too. I worked the second shift, and Dad would pick me up when work was over. One night, I just didn't want to wait, so I decided to walk home. It wasn't that far, but I had to walk through some bad areas.

Halfway home, a guy started to shadow me. I started singing Christian songs and praying like mad. He followed me all the way home, but not until almost on my Dad's doorstep did he come up to me and lay a hand on me. I told him, "Get your damn hands off me." He picked up a fist-sized rock and threw it at me. Fortunately, his aim was as bad as mine. Or could this have been the Lord looking out for me. I rushed inside and told Peter. He looked for the guy, but he was gone.

My next job was on the salad line at a steak house. I rode my bike several miles across town to work the second shift. One day, as I was cycling to work, I got caught in traffic. All the cars were stopped at the light; it was pretty backed up. Well, Miss Know It All figured she could get ahead by inching along the area between the cars and the sidewalk. I was making pretty good progress until some guy's son stuck his arm out of the window of their truck. I was at the back end of the truck, and I lost control of my bike. (Did I tell you I'm not known for my grace?) And wham! down I went, right outside of the passenger's window.

The police officer directing traffic came to check on me. The driver looked, saying nothing. I was relatively unhurt with the exception of bruises the size of huge fists on my thighs, and of course my ego was shot to pieces. Somebody loaded me up on their truck, and I left my bike at a local gas station and went to work. The first thing I did was go into the walk-in freezer and cry.

That bike got me into a lot of trouble. One night, when I was coming home from work, I had my bag on the back of the bike in a carrier. Some guys pulled alongside of me in their car and told me my bag was falling off. Instead of slowing down, I slammed on my brakes. Guess what went flying, and it wasn't the bag. Talk about bruises. Some people never learn.

Shortly after that accident, I stopped on my home to get a drink of water and to settle down. It was at the old Howard Johnson's where I used to work. I ran into some people I had met at church a while back. The church I attended had two meeting places: one in town and one out in the country. I recognized one of the guys. He had been in that particular restaurant when I used to work there. He would come in and order a cup of coffee and sit for a long time, just reading his Bible. Little did I know at the time how he would feature in my life in the near future.

Have I mentioned that I lived right in the middle of the university section—the one I used to party at so fiercely not so long before? Well, one of the homes soon became available for rent. It was right next door to the home where I had lived in the basement. About five of us got together to rent this house. One of the girls had become involved with some students about a block away. Before moving into the house, I used to hang out with her and those guys. They were not Christians and acted accordingly.

Again I was tottering on the edge. I got involved with one of the guys. He made it very clear to me that anything that might occur would mean nothing to him. Talk about walking both sides of the fence. I was barely on the side of God's fence. Old habits die hard.

Unbeknownst to me, a group of Christian friends was praying for me. One was my roommate. I had quit going to that group, but they were aware of what was going on. Well, I turned away from this tottering—I repented—and I quit hanging with those guys.

Alas, my friend ended up running off with one of the guys. The last I heard about her, she had a baby and had come home and asked her father for help. Her baby was around fourteen months. She ended up giving him up for adoption. She just couldn't provide for him, and she wasn't as fortunate as I was to have such a loving, forgiving father.

17
Romance

Well, I continued to attend church. One day, a new guy came. I had seen him before at Howard Johnson's. He was wearing a white suit and was very good-looking. I went up to him after the service and started talking. His name was Kyle.

Shortly afterward, I went to the parent church out in the country to talk with the senior pastor about some bad dreams and to get some counseling. This church met in what used to be a very large house. We had services in what was once a ballroom. A group of people lived upstairs, renting the bedrooms. There was also an apartment where one of the elders and his wife stayed. This would change from time to time as the elders who stayed on-site switched.

Anyway, I ran into Kyle before I met with the pastor, and we chatted for a few minutes. He lived in one of the bedrooms. I razzed him about something, which I am wont to do with people. Upon leaving later that day, Kyle shouted across the parking lot while he was washing his car, "Will you go out with me?"

I said, "Yes."

Real romantic, huh? I was just thrilled someone was

interested in me.

Well, we did go out. And I was enthralled. I have mentioned that I would do almost anything to be accepted and loved. This included being absorbed in another's personality and learning to cater completely to that person's ego. Here was a big-time chance. Kyle had a huge ego and an extremely high opinion of himself. Subconsciously, I knew that if I could get somebody like this to like and accept me, I had arrived.

Unfortunately, this backfires. You find yourself in a trap. You must live your life around this person, and there is never total acceptance of who you are. This kind of person is completely self-centered. As long as you're satisfying that person's needs, things are fine. But step out of that narrow little box the least amount, and the balance is tipped. There is no room to be you. You must be a shadow of this person, reflecting all that he thinks, does, etc.

It would take over ten years for me to realize this. I married Kyle and immediately began having problems. In spite of the fact that I have a personality that wants to please others, I'm still a very independent, stubborn person.

During our first week of marriage, we had some out-of-town guests coming, and Kyle wanted them to stay with us on our wedding night. I appealed to our pastor to intervene. That was the beginning of hell on earth. Although I had been pretty darn wild in the past, I still ruled my own life. I made all the decisions in my life, though they were not always good ones. But I was independent, and I would make it. I had survived a heck of lot and didn't like being told what to do.

At first it was a relief not to have to worry about things. But it soon soured. I still had patterns that had been imbedded in me for quite a few years: my sexual roots, which went far and deep. I had equated sex with love. I still had a very strong sex drive, which in most marriages would be a very welcome addition to the marriage bed. Not so in my life. Kyle's sex drive didn't come close to mine; he was content making love once a week and, if I was lucky, maybe even twice a week.

So I encountered more rejection. And I couldn't believe it. Weren't people supposed to get married and live happily ever after? I had my head in the clouds. No marriage is hunky-dory all the time. We are humans and must learn to adjust to one another, especially in marriage. But I wasn't realistic. Yet I accepted my lot and tried even harder.

Kyle was of the old school that a wife must submit to and obey her husband in all things. He would read the scriptures to me anytime we had a difference of opinion, and in this he would *always* get his way. Didn't he know the Bible better than me? What was wrong with me that I couldn't submit? Thus began the painful groaning and calling out to God to help me submit to this man.

There was no room for any difference of opinion. It seemed I couldn't even have a thought of my own. All my thoughts had to reflect what my husband believed. Many an argument would end up in him saying, "If you can't submit to me and do what I tell you, then you can go home to your dad's." This started in our first year of marriage; it was the beginning of a horrible pattern of tyranny and manipulation. He would get his way no matter what. He would accuse me of being an argumentative woman. He wouldn't ever let up once an argument began. He would badger me until I finally gave in, just to regain a semblance of peace. He would force me to say I was sorry. I would end up doing so because I'd grow sick of the badgering.

But it began a deep resentment. And, of course, I blamed myself. Countless times I would cry to God to help me submit to my husband. But enforced submission is no longer submission. Submission is something done out of the heart. If a husband loves and cherishes his wife as the Bible instructs him to, his wife will go out of her way to please him. Kyle conveniently forgot about this part of the scriptures.

Submission becomes easy and natural if you're both doing what the Bible says. You're both living to please and serve the other person. Kyle never grasped the teaching about serving others: Jesus said He came not to be served but to serve.

Ironically, Kyle wanted to be something in the ministry. He spent many hours studying great men of the past and of modern times. In all his studies, he often missed one of the underlying principles in these men's lives. Yes, they did become famous, and they did do a lot to glorify God's name, but one of the things that they shared was giving in servanthood to others. Kyle missed that part completely. He hardly ever served another person without an underlying motive—usually recognition. "I'm involved in a nursing home ministry. I'm involved in the prison ministry. So why can't people see how great I am. I know the Bible better than most ministers do. I have so much more knowledge than most Christians do." Me, me, me, I, I, I. *Yuck!*

Of course, in the beginning I would defend him. I had to. We had very few friends. The few people who had known us before we got married were more tolerant than others. But as the years went by and we moved, this changed. As did our churches. At some point early on, we quit going to the full-gospel churches we had started out in. One of the key ministers in those churches had been involved in the sin of homosexuality. He was married with two beautiful children, but the lack of checks and balances in his life and no accountability had brought freedoms he couldn't handle. Kyle had greatly admired this man, so it was quite a blow. We moved into another town about two hours away and started attending a Baptist church.

Another fact I failed to mention was Kyle's trouble keeping a job. His condescending, better-than-everyone-else attitude was his downfall. He would give other reasons for why he was looking for another job, and of course I would support him in this. But there were many job changes over the years.

Meanwhile, I began to withdraw further and further. My one way of escape was in reading novels. I would read five or six a week. As time went on, it seemed to be my only way of handling things.

Kyle was an extremely unemotional man. He was rarely affectionate, and 90 percent of the time, I was the one who initiated lovemaking. It was all I could get from him. Even though he was a good lover, it was all very mechanical.

And of course he always did his "scriptures" twice a day. What's wrong with that? It sounds like an excellent thing to do. Yes, it does, but you have to know how it transpired. He didn't just open the Bible and read. He had a large portion of it memorized and would go over it by rote in his mind. He made the Word of God vain repetition. The only difference between him and the followers of Krishna was the sound of the words. It brought no life or fruit, though he would tell you otherwise.

If he had had a hard day at work, it would take him hours to go over those scriptures in his mind. "Don't interrupt me, Chelsea; I'm doing my scriptures" was always his response. Often when he finished, it was late, and he was so burnt out he went to bed. Of course, there was no time for even the shortest of conversations, or he would fall asleep while I was talking to him. Is it any wonder I gained the reputation of talking continuously? I had such a need to talk and to have someone listen to me, it drove me crazy.

Our marriage meant rejection on all sides for me. Not only was I not accepted for who I was, I couldn't even have a thought to myself. And I didn't have anyone to talk to, to share with.

Things went on like this for a long time. They just steadily got worse and worse. I had to account for every moment of my day when I didn't work outside the home. I had to be putting in so many hours doing this or that. I had to work eight hours a day every day. Rules, rules, rules. I was miserable but wouldn't admit it.

After we married, I went back and studied for my GED, since I had dropped out of high school. Then I went to a community college to get an associate's degree in secretarial science. Guess who decided that this was the best course for me to take. It was good for me to go to school, but would I have chosen that field if given the freedom to investigate what would best suit me and my talents? Could I have taken some courses in journalism or drama? Oh well, such is life. At least I learned how to type, but I have never been good at it. My mind races too far ahead of me.

Well, time went on with a vengeance. Soon we decided to start a family. We had put this off until we could be established in our first home. It took almost a year for me to get pregnant, but that's not a surprise in light of our love life. Shortly after that, Kyle again lost his job. That big mouth and argumentative spirit had gotten him in trouble again. It took me years to realize it wasn't me who liked to argue. (He used to accuse me of this, and I bought into it.) He would also get into arguments with his parents. And with me. Yes, I contributed to the arguments because it takes two to tango, but I was not the originator.

This man would not examine himself to see his faults. But it's only when we closely exam ourselves and honestly 'fess up and give these faults to the Lord that can we change. You can't just give it a blanket statement, which is what he would do. That never brought change. How could it when you don't even know what needs to change?

Well, we were certainly in a dilemma. I was pregnant,

with Kyle unemployed and no insurance. Kyle started putting out résumés like mad. We expanded our search area to include the South, since Kyle's parents had moved there. We thought it would be good for us to spend some time around his parents. And lo and behold, he did receive a job offer in the South. The company not only moved us down there, but also took care of all the medical expenses for the baby, even though it was a preexisting condition. What a blessing!

18
Down South

We quickly became involved in the local Baptist church. I had our baby and got involved with the Women's Missionary Union (WMU) in our church. As time went on, we made a few friends. I met a woman who had had a baby right when I did. We enjoyed each other's company, and her husband had had a born-again experience and was pretty tolerant of Kyle's ways. Plus, he too was an engineer, so there was some common ground. But they soon moved back to their hometown.

This left a *huge* gap in my life—until I got involved in a leadership capacity in the WMU. I was the project director for two years in a row. This gave my organizational skills a lot of scope. I learned to get up in front of a congregation of over five hundred and give little "blurbs" about upcoming projects. Of course, I was nervous, but I was able to handle it and even came to enjoy it.

One of the projects we did was Project Angel Tree, in conjunction with the Chuck Colson's Prison Fellowship, which provided Christmas gifts from local churches to children of prisoners. As usual I went about things in a totally different way. I worked with one of the women from the prison ministry, and she was as unorthodox as I. We decided to canvas all the local churches in our state, and we ended up providing gifts for over nine hundred children.

I contacted the churches in my area, no matter what the denomination. This usually took the form of contacting women's groups. We then found out how many "angels" each church wanted. At that point, the church would take over the project. When all the angels were distributed, they would buy gifts for the children. I believe that it was the best Christmas some of these children ever had. People also really enjoyed being a part of it. All the churches in my area brought the gifts to my home to be stored for transport later. Our bonus room was packed. The other woman helped organize a Christmas party downtown. I couldn't attend; guess who wouldn't give me "permission" to go.

I was also involved in teaching conversational English to Japanese women in our area. This was very rewarding. The Japanese people are very gracious and grateful for anything you do for them. This led to me teaching privately. I taught one class on how to make Christmas decorations using goose eggs. Participants would cut the eggs open and fill them with miniature scenes. These scenes varied: nativity scenes, small churches, small Christmas trees, etc. Very few of the women understood English, but it wasn't a problem. There was always someone who had a pretty decent grasp of the language and would interpret. Most of it was hands-on anyway, from the cutting open to the painting to the filling. I loved this and even made a little money on the kits.

But things at home had worsened. Our son was quite a handful. He was very active and often got into trouble. And, as I'm sure you probably already guessed, I had little or no help from his father.

Our church had had an interim pastor, and it was going through a building fund program. So we decided to start looking for another church. I guess these were as good excuses as any to leave, since Kyle couldn't find anyone to take him seriously and continued to alienate people through his condescending attitude. He had no friends; he just couldn't make friends. All he had was his mother and me.

We went to several churches before we settled on one. At that point our marriage was in horrible shape. And we'd had another baby. Of course, this didn't solve our marital problems either. I really wanted to leave Kyle but could see no way out. He was always quick to point out to me that divorce was a grievous sin and only permitted in cases of adultery and of unbelievers yoked to believers.

I even contemplated adultery to make a way out, but I could never bring myself to do it. It was an abhorrent thing to me. I had been faithful all those years and wouldn't start going down that trail. I did go down it in my mind, but it was short-lived because I knew it was just as much a sin in God's eyes to commit adultery in my mind as it was to do it in the flesh—albeit the consequences would be different.

I started thinking about going to the pastor for counseling, which my mother-in-law had been encouraging me to do for years. She knew I was unhappy. And for years I would say I could handle it myself with the Lord's help. We had started attending a full-gospel charismatic church again. As time went on, and as the pastor continued to preach the Word in a way that brought much-needed spiritual food to my soul, I started to contemplate the idea of getting counseling from him. I had never felt that the pastors I'd had were capable, but I was getting desperate. And this pastor seemed to know a lot.

One day I decided to look up the word submission in the dictionary. It stated that it was a voluntary act, one person yielding to another. I hadn't experienced that in our marriage of close to ten years. I realized I had been forced to agree with him, forced to believe what he believed, forced to apologize. Forced, forced, forced. And I had begun to hate him. There was no love left; it had been stamped out, trodden on, and obliterated.

So I finally got up the courage to call the pastor and ask for counseling. He said it would have to be the two of us together. I told him a little about what I had been feeling. I said Kyle would never listen to me.

And I confronted Kyle. He wouldn't admit that there was anything wrong. He just said it was my fault that I wasn't happy and that I had to submit to him anyway. This confrontation happened in a public place, and he insisted I tell him what was wrong. On the way home, I just couldn't stand it. I told him I was leaving. He said,

"Go ahead, but you're not taking the children or anything else with you."

At home I packed a few things, and he tried to take

the checkbook and credit cards from me. He also took my car keys away. I went to the neighbors and called a friend, who came to pick me up. This was only the beginning.

I stayed away overnight, and at that point Kyle agreed to counseling with the pastor. That lasted one session before I went back to him. Of course, Kyle kept up the farce for a few months, but then it was the same old thing: submit, submit, obey, obey, obey. It became very oppressive, as it was just a way of manipulating me in order to get his way. If there was a disagreement, it was my fault.

All the years we were married, I can count on one hand the times he apologized to me, and even then it was because I badgered him to. I have to admit that I had my faults also. I had become a nag. But when I was confronted with that, at least I made an effort to change. Kyle would never admit to being wrong or having any faults.

It wasn't long before old patterns emerged again. I left him again and was gone ten days. I went back under the advice of my pastor, and we started weekly counseling—one of us with the pastor and the other with the women's counselor at our church. During my counseling time, I experienced a lot of pain and growth. I faced a lot of things about myself that were unpleasant; I wanted to change and get rid of those ugly things about myself.

Kyle did make some changes, but they were only surface things. He held deeply entrenched beliefs about marriage, submission, and women in general. He had no respect for anybody. In his mind, he was more spiritual than most—if not all—pastors because he read and meditated on the scriptures more than most pastors. He had such a high opinion of himself, he could not and would not entertain the thought of faults. How sad and sick.

During all those years of marriage, there was no place for me to be able to talk, share my feelings, or just chat. Kyle was too busy meditating on his scriptures. He used this avenue to shut out people and feelings. He had no friends, so we seldom ever had mutual friends. At first we got together with other couples to do things, but over the years that ceased as Kyle alienated people by being condescending.

God was good and always supplied me with one or two very good friends. And I always had my novels to derive some feeling from. More and more, I retreated to reading. I was insatiable. I didn't work outside of the home—no, no, Kyle didn't want that, not until the kids were in school and then only part time. And when Kyle came home from work, he was too busy doing his scriptures to spend any time with the children or me.

I found myself taking things out on my oldest child. I would get angry with him and scream and yell at him. I didn't allow myself to beat him, but I verbally lashed out at him in anger many times. God, in His grace, has drawn us together, but there are times when I look back and shudder at my treatment of my wonderful child.

I was a time bomb waiting to explode. There were so many constraints placed on me in my marriage, and I couldn't see any way out. I knew there were no scriptural grounds for divorce. At times I even contemplated suicide, as it was the only way I could see to get out. But I couldn't do that to my children. Who knows whether I would've taken that way out if I had no children. I talked about it with one of my friends, and she said that my children and I could stay with her family. At least it would be a place to go.

Soon Kyle started the same old song and dance. "We wouldn't have any problems if you'd just submit, Chelsea." But I'd had it. I just couldn't live like that anymore. We had one last session with the pastor. I had a friend watching the boys, the same friend who said we could live with them. This time the boys would be with me. At the end of the meeting, I told Kyle I was leaving him and not coming back. I called my friend and told her Kyle had left and not to be available.

I went back to her house, and a few hours later, guess who showed up. I told him I didn't want to talk to him, and he insisted we at least discuss visitation with the children. He wanted to have them every weekend. I said I'd like to have them at least one weekend a month so I could do things with them. He refused, saying I was being unreasonable and just wanting my way. Of course, he neglected to see who was insisting on his way.

I got angry and ran into the house. He ended up crawling through a window and trying to physically take the children. There were no men in the house, just women and children. I tried to stop him, and he put his hands around my throat, pressing me against a sliding glass door.

My friend called the police after putting back the phone he had torn out of the wall. The police showed up, but what could they do? Kyle left. The pastor came and then went to speak with Kyle. Kyle said he wouldn't pull any more scenes. Not! The very next night he showed up at the care group and grabbed one of the children. The only way he would put Eli down was when I agreed to let him see the children every weekend. To this day, he still sees them every weekend. He seldom does anything with them, but he still insists on seeing them every weekend.

19
Who Am I, Anyway?

So many years of my life had been spent being told by someone or some organization what to do and when to do it that I had a very rude awakening. Although I had many opinions and beliefs, I had almost no freedom to make decisions on my own. Yes, I had many responsibilities. But to actually come up with solutions to problems on my own was not a skill I had been allowed to develop. I was told how to handle things, what job would suit me when the time came, etc.—even to the point of starting a home course on subcontracting in the building industry. Kyle wanted me to take that course so we could "sub out" a new home and go into the building business. I got out of that, but it wasn't easy.

So, what was I going to do now that we were separated? Secretarial work offered very little to someone who couldn't type very fast and had only worked temporary jobs seven years before. Fortunately, I had a friend when I was in Virginia who had started a cleaning business on her own. I stayed in Virginia for seven weeks after leaving Kyle, and I went with her to help clean two of her houses. I liked it very much and kept it in the back of my mind.

I look back and see how hard it was for me to make up my mind about anything at first. One day I would say one thing, and the next day it would be something different. It was definitely like branches waving whichever way the wind blew. One thing I want to instill in my children is the ability to make their own decisions and be responsible for their own actions. Well, my own decision-making process was developing. I was learning to slow down and think more before making a decision. And I certainly prayed for guidance and wisdom.

First things first. When I finally left, I contacted a lawyer to file for separation. I still didn't plan on divorcing Kyle, just on being separated indefinitely. I did want some kind of support and legal standing as far as the children were concerned, so I looked into my legal options. The lawyer wanted $1,500 up front.

The case never went to court, and the lawyer did very little for me. He never gave me a bill itemizing anything and ended up keeping the whole amount. Oh well, live and learn.

My friend did let me and the children come and live with their family. This didn't work out well, since the house was limited on space, and we had two extremely different approaches to raising children. We were even sharing beds, but it was a place to stay, and we tried to make it work.

When I thought I'd be going to court in a few weeks, I decided to visit relatives in Virginia until the court date. When I got there, my cousin graciously offered to put up my children and me indefinitely—or, as she put it, as long as necessary. This was after finding out the court date was a good two months away.

At least we had a place to ourselves. They had two children older than mine. They both worked and needed to replace the combined nanny/housekeeper who was leaving soon. They said I could do that for a time. This worked out well, even though it was a temporary thing.

That's when I slipped back into some old habits. I had picked up drinking again on occasion. Before I left Kyle, I would go over to visit our neighbors and have a drink or two some days. It was a way to handle the horrible mess my life was in—not an answer, just an escape. At my cousin's house, I started drinking again. First it was just a few beers every night, and then it was mixed drinks again.

One night, when everyone was gone but me and my boys, we rented a few movies. I made up a pitcher of margaritas and drank the whole thing myself. It sure felt good, but it was just escaping things again. And I sure had a sore head the next day.

Kyle called and talked to me while I was there, but it always ended up on a bad note. He kept telling my uncle and cousin, "Make her come home." What a joke! During all that time, he didn't send me any money. At one point he offered to send money to my uncle and aunt or my cousin. They all told him the same thing: he should send the money to me. He also made plans to rent a car from there and pick up the boys one weekend so he could take them up to see his brother and family up north.

Well, Kyle did show up and have the weekend with his children and family, which I later found out ended up being a disastrous visit. Our oldest son was completely out of control, ill mannered, and horribly behaved. Their father didn't even try to control him; he just spent his time talking and being out of touch with what his offspring were doing. He became totally oblivious.

When Kyle picked up the boys, he left me a letter. It was one of the sweetest, most beautiful letters he had ever written. He said he would move out of the house, find another place to rent, and we could start counseling again with whomever I chose. He added that the boys and I could move back in, and he would pay the mortgage payment, all the bills, and pay me so much a week.

It did the trick. I decided to try one more time. This was in October, and I had already put my oldest child in school there. We loaded up and went back to the house I had left three months before. You think this might be a great thing? Within weeks we were back to the same old worn-out tune: submit, submit, obey, obey. I said we were wasting the pastor's time. Even during the last session, when Kyle tried to manipulate and the pastor pointed out what he was doing, Kyle denied it.

Kyle stayed in his apartment for a very short period. Weeks before Christmas, he informed me he was moving back into his house and that I didn't have to leave; he wouldn't bother me at all, but he was moving back in. Guess who had dropped her separation suit when she came home and had no legal ground to stand on. I knew this guy would do what he said. What would keep him from breaking in? He had just broken into someone else's house months before. What made anybody think he wouldn't hesitate to break into his own home?

I told my friend about all this and was considering

moving into her garage. I was willing to spend money to have the garage fixed up into two bedrooms. This put me back $5,000— money that was available from a sad circumstance. My father had died in a tragic accident, and there was a wrongful death suit. The money was a long time coming, but it did come.

We discussed the possibility of our staying two years. The money would be rent up front. On looking back, I can't say whether or not I had any other choice. Kyle was ready to move in immediately, and he would have. Would we still be alive at this point if I had dug in my heels and not left? Only God knows. Maybe he was just bluffing, but I had pulled out all the stops and taken away the position he had of totally controlling my life. He thrived on the control thing, and I had given him that place for ten years. I thought it was the right thing at first but soon found out it wasn't. So two days before Christmas, my sons and I moved into our new "home."

Ten months was as long as we could stay there. There were too many differences, and trying to blend eight people in one home was no easy task. Meanwhile, I had started a cleaning business a month before I moved into my friend's home. It started out slowly, and I had a lot to learn, but I enjoyed it thoroughly. It was a treat to go clean where there was no one around. It afforded me some privacy and peace and quiet, which were scarce in a home shared by so many people.

20
Independence and Freedom

Whenever I lived with others, I always hoped to be in a place of my own. I had been looking off and on at mobile homes—singlewide, doublewides, new, old, and repossessed. I felt that if I could get into a place and pay cash for it, it would give me a lot of financial freedom. There's nothing like living mortgage-free, which was my goal and desire.

At first I looked at new places. It was great, but I would still have to put out a lot in monthly payments. And I had to figure in a monthly lot rent. I just wasn't making that much on a regular basis, so looking at repossessed mobile homes became more and more appealing. In addition to all of this, Kyle was saying he was going to divorce me, since I wouldn't come back to him. I told him he had to do what he had to do. I wouldn't fight it. So there would be some monetary settlement there.

The Lord opened the door one day. I found a ten-year-old doublewide for sale at a great price. I ended up putting some money into it to fix it up because it was in pretty bad shape. The floors had holes in them in some places, and the carpet had seen better days. It ended up looking a lot different when I was finished. All this occurred in a matter of a week. I had a carpenter and a plumber working, and I painted the kitchen myself, which is very obvious. A friend of mine wallpapered another part of the kitchen for me. What a wonderful blessing! And guess what. No mortgage payment!

The first weekend in my new place, I just stayed at home, relishing the peace and quiet. When I had been married, I'd had a lot of privacy—too much. But going from one extreme to another was a big adjustment. For a long time, I was very content to stay at home on weekends when the boys went to their father's. I derived so much pleasure from just cleaning my own place. It was all mine. What an incredible gift!

I continued to clean houses, which I had been doing for almost a year. When I cleaned, I paid someone to take care of my youngest son. I'll never forget what he told me one of the times I went to pick him up. The woman had taken him with her to the mall, and he said he'd tried to keep up with her. But she was very tall and his body didn't even come close. He was only around three or four and wouldn't get his height until well into the future. There are still some funnies out there.

I thought it might be good to have something lined up for the time when the boys went to live with Kyle for his year. That was part of the joint custody agreement that Kyle had worked up. One parent would have the children during the week, and the other parent would have them on the weekends, and at the end of the year we would switch. I just didn't want to fight with him, so I agreed to it. It could have been worse, and I had hopes that Kyle would change his mind when his year arrived.

The Lord continued to reveal things to me and to show me areas of my life that needed changing. It has been an ongoing process. I remember my counselor telling me that we go from glory to glory. As we grow as Christians, we move to the place along the way where we no longer are happy with business as usual. We want to grow and move on. This is something I wanted with a passion. I am an all-or-nothing person, and this extended into my Christian walk. I was discovering new and wonderful things about the Lord all the time and was eager to grow. Many times I felt that God was far away from me, but I was so determined to lay hold of Him that I never quit or gave up. I had moments of dry wilderness, but most of the time it was a rich experience to discover more and more about Jesus and His rich love toward me.

Well, Kyle's year finally rolled around, and he had not changed his mind. He was working from his house at the time, and it being summer, he had the boys. What a mess! Many times he wouldn't feed them until ten or eleven at night, and then it would be doughnuts. If the boys complained, he would yell at them that he was doing his scriptures and that they had to leave him alone.

Luke, my oldest, was eight years old and was allowed to ride his bike anywhere he wanted to. His father was unaware of where he was most of the time. He took the nonchalant attitude that Luke would show up sometime. One day, Luke showed up at my place—six miles away. He had ridden his bike much of the way on a busy highway. I called his father and asked if he knew where Luke was.

His response was "Somewhere out on his bike."

Needless to say, I prayed a lot about my children and tried to release them into the Lord's hands. Sometimes I succeeded, and sometimes I didn't. During all that time, I remained on a friendly basis with my former in-laws. They understood why I couldn't live with their son anymore.

During one summer, the Lord intervened. My mother-in-law and father-in-law called me, and we had a three-way conversation. Kyle was about to invite a man he had met only once at a Benny Hinn conference to live with him and the boys. This man would function as a nanny, and Kyle would help him out by sending him to school. The three of us were very upset. They wanted to know what I could I do about it. The only thing they knew about him was what Kyle had told them: he was on a drug called lithium, and he'd had a drug problem in the past. And his parents had kicked him out.

It's all well and good to accept people as new creatures in Christ, but let's not put them in charge of your children when you have very little information about them. I wrote a letter, pointing out these things to Kyle and even going as far as saying maybe this guy had a problem with molesting children in the past and he might even have AIDS. I commended Kyle on the fact that he wanted to help this guy out, but I made it very clear it would not be at the expense of our children. This guy could backslide into old ways that he had never even revealed to Kyle.

This did stop Kyle, but it was a close call. The timely intervention of the Lord helped us to deal with the situation. When I sent my father-in-law a copy of the letter, his comment was that it sounded like a lawyer wrote it. That's because the greatest advocate in the world led me when I wrote it.

Not too long afterward, I found out Kyle had resorted to some other unsafe practices with the children. He had our eight-year-old babysitting his four-year-old brother for four and five hours at a time. Alone. So that their father could go out on a date. This happened a few times. Again I had to confront him, but God continued to give me the grace to deal with those crazy situations. And as I've grown, the Lord has helped me to keep anger out of it.

Meanwhile, a part of me was so deeply imbedded that I didn't recognize it for a long time. The desire to please people was still there, entwined with the feeling that I wasn't acceptable to others. I had to perform, to do things, to be a certain way for others to accept me. That's why I had been drawn to Kyle, who was very performance-oriented in his giving of love. Unfortunately, the performance that he demanded was impossible for me to live under. A perfectionist and a legalist is never satisfied with what you do.

In spite of all this, I still wanted to be married again—to the "right" person. I was chomping at the bit, as the saying goes. My pastor wanted me to wait at least a year before even thinking about dating, and I unwillingly agreed to that. He had always been there for me, and I looked to him as my covering, now that I wasn't married. Yes, the Lord is my ultimate covering, but He does place shepherds in the body to guide the sheep. I accepted what my pastor asked, but it was an unwilling submission. I just went through the motions. It had become such a habit over the years.

I did go to the singles care group for four or five months—until a guy gave me more attention than I could handle. I was so immature; I couldn't handle attention from men in the balanced way.

I was still a little girl wanting to please; I wasn't seeing straight. I was still going to counseling. I had to have someone to unload with, to sort things out with. I was going through so many changes. I told her about my feelings, which she passed on to the pastor. It was decided that I should go to a married care group. I was so mad about this. They told me it was just like lining me up in the scope of a Satan's rifle. Of course, this was true, but it took me a long time to admit it.

I took a course in WordPerfect to be in a better position to look for a job that would include benefits and some stability. But I can't say that I ever prayed about that decision; I just decided on my own that it was the right thing to do. I sent out a lot of résumés and went on quite a few interviews. But my lack of experience and slow typing speed kept me from getting any decent offers. But one interviewer was impressed with my knowledge; I had done better on a test than anyone.

One day I was offered a position downtown. It looked like it had potential for growth, and I was willing to give up most my cleaning jobs to try it. I kept some of my clients, who were willing to let me clean in the evening hours. I just couldn't let go of my cleaning altogether.

The position downtown lasted all of two weeks.

I wasn't cutthroat enough to make it there. In many ways, I was just an innocent, willing to think the best of everybody. That's not the way it is in the world, and this came as quite a blow to me.

I decided that the clerical field wasn't for me. I thought maybe waitressing would pay off, even though it had been fifteen years since I had done it. I got a job at a local Italian restaurant. The boss that hired me was a man a little younger than me. All the other staff were in their late teens to mid-twenties, so I had more in common with him.

I slipped into my old ways of "turning it on" where men are concerned. I can't fully explain this aspect of myself. For years I had sent out the signals big-time, and the response was always obvious. I can't tell you exactly how I would go about this, but the consequences for a born-again Christian single woman were sometimes disastrous.

On one hand, I would operate how I had in the past, and on the other hand, I would let people know I was a Christian. Needless to say, my boss found me to be a mystery, as there were so many conflicting signs. I started to recognize this about myself and asked the Holy Spirit to help me stop every time I started doing it. I remember telling a friend about it. He was married, and he and his wife were good friends of mine. He said he had never seen me do that, and I told him he had just not had eyes to see that side of me.

Well, the job at the Italian restaurant wasn't paying well. We just didn't have that much business during the hours I worked. I had started cleaning a little more, and this helped to supplement my income. Then the woman I used to work for when I was pregnant with my second child called me one day out of the blue to see if I would be interested in working for her for a few months. I went back to work there and continued to serve my own cleaning clients. At one time I was cleaning several houses a week and putting in close to forty hours a week in my temporary job. But it was good. The children were with their father, and I had plenty of time on my hands. Going back to work was a real blessing for me financially, even if it was only for a short time. It was also quite an adjustment.

I am a very people-oriented person; I can get along with almost anyone. But I sometimes had run-ins with aggressive people, as my personality is very strong. And the stress in that place when I first started was unreal; they were all extremely behind in their work. My job was the same as it had been for a few years, but now it was all computerized. I didn't feel I could ask too many questions because of the stress level. Add to this the fact that I talk to myself incessantly when dealing with problems, and I'm unaware that I'm muttering to myself.

At the end of the first week, I had a chat with my boss, and she asked me to be little quieter. Argh! I couldn't ask for help, and I couldn't talk to myself while working. But I did try hard to adjust and quiet down.

When things settled down a bit there, I sometimes lightened things up. My boss knew I was a bit of a cut-up, and I would razz her every now and then. One day she said my shoes made too much noise when I walked. They didn't have carpet, as it was a roofing company, which meant people tracked in a lot of asphalt. I just looked at her and did a little tap dance. It certainly made her think about how absurd she was being. And we had a good chuckle.

Laughter has always been one of my ways of dealing with things. The older I get, the more I laugh. Life is too short to be serious all the time.

21
Romance Again

My other job duties were doing general secretarial work and being a receptionist. Often I would be up front when new applicants and visitors from other plants came. Of course, salesmen did too, and on occasion they were obnoxious. One of the salesmen stands out in my mind. My boss had gone out to lunch, and I was feeling disgruntled. He came up to the window and asked for my boss. I told him she was at lunch and would be back soon, and he could have a seat and wait.

Then he came through the back. I thought, Who does this short guy think he is? I don't recall how things went the way they did, but we ended up cutting up and laughing a lot. He had an outrageous personality. I could really play off him, and him off me. That day I was not guarding myself as far as putting out vibes. After he left, he called me and asked me out on a date. I said no and told him I wasn't interested.

Several weeks passed, and he asked me again. I told him I'd have to pray about it. And I meant it. I was almost at the end of my year of no dating, so I ran it past my pastor. He said, "As long as you keep your head together, it will be fine." Little did my pastor know that was I incapable not only of keeping my head together, but also of keeping my flesh in order. Of course, I didn't admit this to myself. No way. I wanted to start dating so bad that I wouldn't even consider any parameters. I thought, *Of course I can keep it together. I'm a grown woman, aren't I?*

I had weekends off at the time. Just three months after Kyle had the boys full time during the week, he had approached me about switching back. He was looking for full-time employment; his at-home business hadn't panned out. He knew he couldn't work downtown or anyplace within commuting distance and still pick up the boys from the afterschool program on time. Of course, I agreed, not quite willingly. I had to play the game and make him think I'd do it grudgingly. If he thought I was eager to have the children back, the chances were he wouldn't approach me about taking care of them again.

Well, the salesman and I started going out after Thanksgiving that winter. No longer was I the cool customer this guy had seen when he came into the plant. I had reverted to sending the signals again. Instead of going to my counselor and sharing what I was going through, I decided I was a big girl and could handle things on my own. It's not like she wanted to control me or have me depend on her. She just knew a lot about me and how truly vulnerable I was.

As I look back, it saddens me that I basically flipped my nose at my pastor and my counselor. My attitude was "I'll show you I can do this on my own." It was the attitude of a little girl, a child. I allowed myself to be set up and had no one to blame for the things that happened but myself. And believe me, I did.

The first time or two that we went out, this guy didn't know that he had a bomb on his hands—a sex bomb. He didn't have to do anything at all, because I was constantly turned on. Even today, that is very hard to admit. I found I couldn't stop or say no, just like the long-ago past. *What am I doing? Why am I in this position?*

The Lord tried to give me obvious ways out. I could have severed the relationship and gone about my business. Instead, I tried to play the game. This was the first approach: *Okay, we'll not do such and such physically.* But it wouldn't stay that way when we were together. Things moved along too rapidly. That's the way this guy operated: fast and smooth.

Then we thought we were in love. *Will you marry me?* That way the things we were doing could be justified. And he had shared with me that he had been a lay minister in the past. *Why don't we say our vows and live as husband and wife when we're together on weekends, since I was spending it at his house anyway.*

For a while I was euphoric. But it wasn't complete. I knew I had betrayed the trust of my pastor and counselor. The life I was living wouldn't hold water. I knew a time of reckoning was fast approaching. And, of course, I was starting to see things about this guy that even I couldn't overlook. I'm extremely accepting of others; there is very little that bothers me. I'm very difficult to offend or hurt. I just take things as they happen and often don't even recognize slights and innuendos. In spite of this, some things I couldn't overlook, accept, or begin to like about this man.

Then the shocker of my life happened: I was pregnant. We had been very careful, and it shouldn't have happened. But God has a purpose in everything that happens in our Christian life. We had planned to get married in July so that we could ease into things, but we quickly rescheduled the wedding to a few weeks away. I set up an appointment to meet with my counselor. It was very difficult. Gosh, she knew me so well. I told her everything. She said she'd get Simon, my pastor, up-to-date, and I would meet with him and my intended husband. I left feeling about as big as a worm.

When I talked with Hank, his attitude was the same: "We didn't do anything wrong, and our vows are valid in God's sight." But God will not put His stamp of approval on fornication, no matter how we try to dress it up.

I met with Simon privately and will never forget that moment. It was if I had stabbed him in the back. He was hurt because I was one of his sheep. *Well,* I thought, *he's just upset* because he looks at me like a daughter, and *I cheated him out of the opportunity to be a part of this.* Poppycock! When one of the fold acts irresponsibly and flips her nose at the wise counsel given, it hurts. Simon said he would not be able to support me in my marriage, and if I went through with it, I would no longer be under his covering as my shepherd. This was a hard thing for me to face.

Hank had his say with the pastor in a joint meeting of my counselor, Simon, and the two of us. I had very little to say, and when it was all over, Hank said very defensively, "Well, that's my dog-and-pony show." It was the beginning of the week, and I was determined to go through with our wedding on Saturday. But things were not looking good.

Hank came over that Wednesday night, and I just wasn't with it. I had felt unsettled the weekend before all this and had been snappy with him. I blamed it on the pregnancy hormones, which he was willing to accept. I knew this man really didn't want a baby, but he wouldn't admit it. (He was twelve years older than me.) But we had spent a lot of time talking about our future. This included a lot of traveling on weekends when the boys were at their father's house. And we would sell my doublewide and use the money to pay off his ex-wife on her part of the equity in their home and to fix up the house. We'd use my child support money to pay certain bills, etc. In other words, I would lose my hard-earned freedom, and he would gain a lot in addition to an unplanned child.

When I first went to his office to meet some of his coworkers, it seemed like a lot of people knew about the baby. He had bragged about the pregnancy without consulting me. And one of his daughter's friends had been told also. *Just how many people has he told?* I wondered. *And don't I have any say in this.* No, it didn't make me very happy at all.

On the day we went to get our marriage license came another big eye opener. I knew Hank had an outrageous personality, but there are limits. He really went to town with some very out-of-line comments, and the woman who filling out our papers made the comment, "Better you than me." I was very bent out of shape.

22
Eye Opener

On the Thursday before the wedding, I was scheduled to clean for some close friends. When I shared the news with them, one reply tipped me over the edge: "If you marry this man just because you're pregnant, you'll have to stay with him. Marriage is a very serious thing in God's eyes. Even if you go through with your pregnancy and give this baby up for adoption, it is a nine-month commitment, not a lifetime commitment, as marriage is." I had considered adoption as an option initially, but Hank wouldn't hear of it. We would get married and raise this child.

When my friends left so that I could clean the house, I was alone. I knew things were bad, though I wouldn't admit it. But God did something He had never done to me in my entire Christian walk. I had been walking with the Lord for sixteen years and had been through hard times with my marriage and subsequent divorce. And I had always experienced God's peace in my life. That day He took the peace away. It was horrible! I wept as I cleaned. I finally cried out, "Okay, God, I won't go through with this marriage!"

Sometimes the Lord does things to get our attention. And He certainly got my attention when He withdrew

His peace that day. I had taken it for granted for sixteen years. Never again. At times, I haven't felt close to the Lord. This was not His fault. We can't base our Christian walk on feelings, which too often betray us. I base my Christian walk on the Word of God. He tells me in His Word that He loves me more than I can imagine. I don't need to give in to feelings of self-hatred or inferiority or to take stock in them. Feelings are great. God made us to have them, but they won't rule my life.

I immediately called Georgeanne to give her the news. She was so relieved. She said she knew the Lord would come through and that she would pass along the news to the pastor. Later she told me that one of our assistant pastors had said that he would have a few choice words to tell me if I went through with the marriage. God is faithful and kept me from making a major mistake. But I was always living close to the edge, and that was not the way I wanted to continue.

I still had to confront Hank. I had to tell him not only that I couldn't marry him but also that I didn't want to see him again. Simon, my pastor, offered premarital counseling with us if I wanted to get married later. But I knew I just couldn't marry this man. So I made it clear to Hank. Or at least I thought I did, but he wouldn't give up.

We had another four-way meeting, and I told him to his face. It was just sex to me, and I wasn't interested. I wasn't quite that blunt, but the idea was clear. I said I did what I felt I had to to justify my actions. It was no fun at all to have to come out and say those things, revealing an unpleasant side of myself, but it was the truth. I knew Simon and Georgeanne still loved me anyway, which made it easier to confess those things.

Hank couldn't accept it. He continued to make appointments with Simon, who would meet with him. But my mind was made up. I wouldn't change it for anything this guy could supposedly do. It got to the point that Simon would cancel appointments with him because nothing changed. He suggested Hank go to the church he used to be affiliated with and find support there.

Finally, Simon asked me to meet with Hank one more time and tell him again. I said, "Fine, when do you want to meet in the office?" He then told me he wanted me to meet with Hank privately. Argh! That was the last thing I wanted to do. But I agreed and set up a meeting in a public place—at a mall food court, right before church.

He proceeded to tell me how much he cared about me. I told him, "It's over. You need to get on with your life. I don't love you."

He said, "Why don't you let somebody love you?" He even implied Simon agreed with that statement.

I said, "You're wrong. I've talked with Simon, and that's not what he said. And furthermore, I don't like you misconstruing things or trying to use Simon to get me back." I told him to leave Simon out of it and that I didn't like his methods. I was mad but wouldn't add sin to my anger by telling him what I really thought of him.

His response was "Do you understand the concept of reaping and sowing? You're going to reap a lot for what you've done to me."

I just looked at him and said, "I am reaping; I'm pregnant." That was the last I saw of the man, but it wasn't the end of his involvement in my life.

23
Choices

Okay, so now I had another decision to make. Our church was very involved in the pro-life movement. Several families functioned as foster parents, and there had been several adoptions. My exposure to adoption had been very positive. I was already a single mom of two wonderful little boys and had functioned that way even when I was married. Did I want the responsibility of raising another child when my other two demand a lot of time and energy?

So I definitely had to pray about adoption, which would be a life-changing decision. I thought about all the factors involved in parenting and adoption. Many things came into that process. One of the biggest factors was the fact that I wanted this child to have a normal life—or at least as normal as can be in this world of sin we dwell in.

I had wanted so much to have that in my own life. It had been an all-consuming desire at one point. Before my first marriage, I thought getting married would meet that desire. Far from it! Such is life. But I knew this baby might have the kind of life I had so wanted for my two sons and myself.

My sons don't have a father that takes much interest in them, apart from viewing them as his possessions. He does love them as much as he's able to. But both of them know without a doubt that he's not a "daddy."

I look at some of my friends and see their family life. One friend stands out in my mind. They have it all: a good marriage and a wonderful family. I admire them. Since we're very good friends, she sometimes tells me about problems they have, but they work through them and have a strong family. I wanted to give my baby this chance, so I decided to go with an adoption plan.

Now that I had an answer to my prayer about the future of this child, I needed to decide which route to take. I'd had wonderful exposure to Bethany Christian Services through my church. I also had my former brother-in-law in mind. I told my former mother-in-law, since we were still close. After she got over the shock of me being pregnant and finished telling me how stupid I was, which I fully agreed with, we discussed my options. She knew I would never consider abortion, and she said, "I know who would take this baby."

"So do I," I replied. She contacted my former brother-in-law, and he eagerly agreed to adopt my child. But I had not quite made up my mind. I needed to pray before making a decision. Deciding where this child would grow up would be one of the most important decisions I would ever make. I knew my brother-in-law and his wife would be good parents, and they did go to church. But what kind of relationship did they have with the Lord? I believed they were saved, but was it evident that they had a personal walk with Jesus? I just wasn't sure.

They dealt with adoptive parents who are committed and active Christians. It's one of the requirements of signing up with them. I wanted my child to have a godly father and mother, so I contacted the agency to discuss all my options—and thus began a new friendship. The woman who came to talk with me was their pregnancy counselor. I told her I was undecided about which route to take: my brother-in-law or their agency. If I did go with their service, it would be because of the positive experiences with them I'd seen at my church. They placed no pressure on me.

My temporary job had ended at the beginning of the year, and I had started to expand my housecleaning slowly. I knew I wasn't in the position to look for another job in light of my pregnancy. Over time, I informed my clients about my condition. It in no way affected my services, since I had started charging by the job instead of hourly. Toward the end of my pregnancy, I slowed down a bit. I cleaned through my seventh month and a little beyond, until it became too much.

In light of the fact that I didn't know enough about my brother-in-law and his walk with the Lord, I decided to go with the adoption agency. My former mother-in-law accepted the decision, but she said, "We will see what we will see," as she always did.

Though I would have gotten financial assistance from my in-laws if I'd chosen to keep the baby in the family, I had prayed and felt the Lord led me to go with the agency. I was learning not to vacillate but to stand firm in what the Lord was leading me to do. I also felt the Lord impress upon me that my brother-in-law and his wife would get a baby.

At one point, my brother-in-law had asked me to pray about being a surrogate with his seed. I had actually thought about it, but I knew I couldn't go through this again. He seemed to accept my decision but, unknown to me, he was still hoping I might change my mind.

Before I decided to go with an adoption, I kept thinking I was carrying a girl. But when I was still with I had the Lord told me I was carrying a son. There were a lot of things I felt the Lord was telling me. As I turned my back on that relationship, I also turned my back on what I thought of the Lord telling me things; I had begun to doubt my ability to hear from Him. I knew I had been playing games with myself and this "speaking from the Lord" had been part of it. So I convinced myself that this child was a girl.

For example, the pregnancy was different. I was sick and had never been sick with my boys. Maybe this was part of God's grace. If I'd known the baby was a boy, there's a good possibility he would've stayed in the family. The appeal of financial support and a possible good used car would have been too much. So who knows? It could have been the Lord letting me go along thinking that I had a girl.

I had many hard months ahead. I had made plans even before I contacted the adoption agency. I had gone to the health department to have another pregnancy test at the request of my counselor because she couldn't believe I was really pregnant. The test was positive, and they set my due date. The health department informed me I was eligible for Medicaid, which would cover all the medical expenses for the doctor and hospital. I kept this in mind. The nurse gave me a list of the doctors in the area who accepted Medicaid, and there was a familiar name on the list: the group I had gone to with my last pregnancy, when I was married.

I set up my first appointment. Because I had gotten a handle on my weight when I moved into my own place, I had lost around twenty-five pounds. I didn't start showing until well into my fifth month. I asked my doctor what I had weighed in my last pregnancy at the same time, and he said I was twenty pounds heavier. I was in the habit of watching what I ate, and I followed through during my pregnancy. It was just another sign of God's grace in my circumstances.

24
Growing Up

One day, I stopped at Georgeanne's on my way home after cleaning. As we sat around chatting, I told her about my youngest son, who was very silly sometimes, as five-year-olds tend to be. He liked to make people laugh. I said that I'd gotten attention in the same way, and for me it was usually in a positive way. Georgeanne said I was a clown in the good sense of the word.

We proceeded to discuss other things, one of which was a topic that had come up at a weekly women's Bible study I had been attending. One of the women was seeking the gift of discernment, something I had never actively sought after, though I knew I was lacking it big-time. This all linked to my desire to be accepted by others; I would accept people as they were—often in a blind, gullible, naive way. Being so desperate for acceptance, I didn't allow myself to see people clearly. This was a great setup for pain because people took advantage of me. It was almost as if I was afraid to see people clearly. I was trusting everyone at face value.

This is what children do, but it's not a great trait in an adult. There's nothing wrong with trusting people, but trust needs to be earned. I would give trust to anybody and then be hurt and rejected. I confessed out loud to Georgeanne that I knew it was time for this little girl to grow up. I decided then and there that I would ask the Lord to help me grow up and to create in me a discerning spirit. I wanted to be more perceptive and not to depend on others' perceptions but on my own.

God, in His grace, did a quick work in me over the next few months. I can't exactly say how it came about, but it did. I still accept people as they are, but my trust has to be earned. I learned that the hard way. Growing up was very painful at times, but it was worth it.

Many other things happened to me during that time. Some of it was quite funny. One day I was cleaning house. The owner, Kiah, kept about twenty horses. Usually she wasn't there when I cleaned. She told me that if any of the horses looked really sick, I should call the vet.

Well, one day I glanced out the glass door and noticed a tiny horse was loose. There were several fields separated by electric fence. This little horse was running after the stallion, who had been by himself in the field closest to the house.

Even with my limited knowledge of horses, I knew this could be a dangerous situation. I scrounged around until I came up with the vet's phone number. The vet's receptionist said she'd page him. She also agreed with me that I couldn't leave the little horse with the stallion. She said I could possibly put him in the barn there.

You never saw anything so crazy. I was five months pregnant, wearing yellow rubber gloves, a bright red shirt, white shorts, and flip-flops. That little horse ran through wire after wire, knocking them all down, from one field to the other. All the other horses flaked out and ran after it. I was so afraid the little horse was going to get hurt.

At one point the little horse got stuck on part of the fence. I untangled him and kept trying to catch him, even to the point of being out with all the full-grown horses. Believe me, I was praying big-time. That little horse ran all over the place and ended up back in the stallion's field, tangled in the wire. This time I was determined to hold on to the tiny thing, and I finally untangled him. Then I half dragged, half carried him into the barn, put him in one of the stalls, and closed the door. I called the vet's office to report my success, and they said the vet would stop by.

I had tried to put the electric wires back as best as I could, but I couldn't put them all back. I was exhausted. Not only had I cleaned up the house, but I had spent two hours trying to deal with that little horse. The vet had shown up two hours after I left.

Kiah later told me that the little horse was a foal—a girl horse—that had been born fifteen minutes before I first saw her and had somehow gotten separated from her mother. She ended up being in that stall alone for three hours, until Kiah came home. The vet didn't even try to get her back with the mare; Kiah later told me that many times a mare will reject her foal in that kind of circumstance. I prayed that the Lord would take care of that little foal and reunite her with her mother, and that the mare would accept her.

Poor Kiah came home to a colossal mess. All the horses had been wandering around, and even her neighbors came over to help deal with it. Some of the horses were injured as a result of this catastrophe, so Kiah incurred additional vet bills. But she still had me come back to clean for her. I have many other cleaning stories, but none quite as crazy as that one.

During my sixth month of pregnancy, I was changing the sheets on my boys' bunk beds. I had put it off far too long. I brought the kitchen chair in to do the top bunk. As I leaned over to pull down the far corner of the fitted sheet—*wham!*—it was like someone had jerked the chair out from under me. I went flying across the room and landed on my hand with a crash and then on my back. I was soon crying, and my oldest son came in to check on me. Miraculously, I hadn't landed on my belly and was unhurt except for a sore hand. Satan would have loved to destroy the baby inside of me, but the Lord had placed guardian angels around me to protect me.

My ex-husband, Kyle, remarried at the end of January—on the date I had originally planned to marry Hank. (How crazy if we'd had the same wedding date! But the Lord in His mercy kept me from making that mistake.) When I met his new wife, I found her to be very nice and friendly. She wanted to talk to me about Kyle, and I would often find myself saying negative things about him. It always got back to him. I also had caught myself explaining to people why I was divorced, what he had been like and done, etc. Afterward I would ask myself, *Why did you say that?* It never felt right.

So I decided I had to quit. It was certainly not pleasing to the Lord to let all that negative stuff keep coming out of my mouth. Thereafter, when I went to pick up the children, I didn't indulge in that crummy behavior. I would just tell Deborah that I had decided not to speak negatively about Kyle.

I failed to mention that he decided once he got married that he wanted to have the children back with him to finish out his remaining year. They went back a few days after he and Deborah got married. He didn't even consult his new wife about it, but that is his way.

At first, the boys were crazy about this woman in their lives. During the month or so that they dated, she had gone all-out, including the boys and wooing them too. It didn't bother me much that the boys preferred to live with their father in light of the circumstances. They were enthralled, but this soon began to wear off.

Kyle and Deborah had marital problems right from the beginning. Although he seemed to have changed in some ways, there were some areas that were completely unchanged, and he began to sing the same old tune to his new wife. She was older when they got married—not a nineteen-year-old—so I thought things would be different. Alas, some things just don't seem to change.

In May, after a big fight between Kyle and Deborah, something happened with my son Luke. He had been given permission to ride his bike to school if he returned immediately afterward. Deborah called me and said he hadn't shown up at four. School was out at two thirty, and he'd had ample time to get home. I said I'd wait a little while and check with her again. After all, it was Friday, and the boys were due to come home with me.

Well, he still wasn't home, so I went over there. Kyle had been contacted and would be home shortly. I got on the phone to call people I thought Luke might have gone to see. There were very few, since he didn't make friends easily. Kyle came home, and we mentioned some places he could check. I got in touch with the school to find out if Luke had even shown up that day. At least we would know how long he had been missing.

The later it got, the more Deborah and I were leaning toward calling the police. Kyle wasn't too keen on that idea, but we put in the call anyway. When the police showed up to make a report and get the pertinent information, Kyle wouldn't even come downstairs. He was upstairs doing his scriptures. It was left to his new wife and his ex-wife to deal with it.

Deborah gave all the information she had and went outside. The officer asked me if there was anything else he should know. I told him he had put me in an awkward position by asking that question, but I proceeded to tell him of Kyle and Deborah's big argument the night before. He said that if Luke didn't show up by dark, they would send out people to look.

A friend of mine had sighted Luke at Big Star. She said he was on his bike and looked sad, like he was running away. I quickly went there and informed the police. It was almost dark, and they were about to start their after-dark search. Moments later, Deborah drove up with Luke in the car. He had been riding his bike toward home. His story was that someone had stolen his backpack with all his Easter candy in it, and since he was going to use it for food, he was going back home.

Deborah thought he should be whipped. Kyle wouldn't even accept the fact that Luke had tried to run away, and he was talking to him upstairs. Luke said something about Deborah beating him, so he was running away. Deborah became livid and denied it, and she asked me to defend her to Kyle. I stayed out of it. I finally went upstairs and told Kyle it was Friday and I was taking the boys for the weekend. Enough was enough.

Shortly after this incident, at Bible study, a leader asked if anybody needed prayer. I brought up the incident and said I wanted prayer in dealing with the crazy situation. It was then that the Lord began the wonderful process of setting me free from worrying, fretting, and holding on to my children. There was very little I could do about what happened when the boys were at their father's, but I was driving myself crazy anyway. The Lord told me that He had them in His hands and was in control, and that I was to let go and let Him take care of them. What a blessed relief!

Well, Mother's Day came, and it was a very significant Mother's Day for me. Billingsly had been given the whole church service. A skit about a young woman choosing adoption over abortion was performed, and I sat up front to get a good view. It brought a few tears to my eyes. Then the birth mother who the skit was based on got up to share. She mentioned that the hardest thing to do was leave her baby in the hospital. At that point I regretted sitting up front. It was all I could do to keep from sobbing uncontrollably. My day to do the same thing was fast approaching. I didn't control my tears, but I made as small a scene as possible.

25
A New Family

I still had a major decision to make. Where would this child grow up? Which family would have the great joy of receiving a child that they had prayed for earnestly? So many people want babies but just can't have them. But just as the Lord had been faithful to lead and guide me that far, I knew He would also lead me to the perfect choice for this little child.

Jenny had been visiting me regularly, and she mentioned the profile book to me. A profile book consists of letters and pictures from prospective adoptive parents. Once you find someone you're interested in, you can then review a more-detailed autobiography of the couple. I looked through this book, but no one stood out. I was drawn to some, but before I could make a firm decision, other birth mothers chose them.

But I still had plenty of time. Jenny continued to come see me regularly. We would just chat about the crazy things that were occurring in my life.

Time went on, and I still hadn't found adoptive parents. Jenny sent me information on other couples, but I wasn't taken by any I saw. Then one day she mentioned some adoptive parents almost ready to be added to the profile book. She also told me about a pastor and his wife that were new in the book. But I knew that was not the life I wanted for my child. Satan attacks those in the ministry even more viciously than us peons.

Jenny said that this other couple hadn't finished their home study but had a church background similar to mine. This sounded promising. I looked through their pictures, and I just knew that these were the people I wanted to raise my child. They already had one biological son, who was fourteen, but they had been unable to have any other children. They had tried adopting three times, but all of them had fallen through. But they felt the Lord wanted them to keep trying. A friend of theirs had told them about Billingsly, and they had investigated.

The first of July, my day to get my children back full time, was fast approaching. I wanted to set up a meeting with the adoptive parents as soon as possible. To avoid a weekend meeting, I wanted to meet with them soon, even though they hadn't finished their home study. Miriam, the woman who dealt mostly with the adoptive parents, wanted to put the meeting off to a later date. So we found a place right in the middle. There are things I drag my feet on, and this wasn't one of those things.

Our first meeting took place at the Billingsly offices, and Georgeanne went with me at my request. I trusted her judgment, and she had been walking with me in this and other things for quite a while. I had prayed and asked the Lord to lead and guide me. I didn't get nervous until we got out of the car. At first it was a little awkward. Keith and Amber were completely bowled over—not by me but by the speed in which things were happening. They had just barely finished their home study and didn't even have a letter prepared for the profile book. I guess I would have been overwhelmed too.

They brought lots of pictures, as I had told Jenny that I wanted to see more. It gave me a glimpse into their lives that only pictures could give. During our meeting, I ended up mentioning the sex of the baby. Jenny had said it would be all right. I had thought that since they already had a son, they would want a daughter. When I asked them about this, they said they would be happy with whatever sex the baby was, so I told them it was a boy. Amber said her son, Christopher, had told them to sprint to the phone when and if they found out the sex; he wanted a brother big-time.

It amazed me that the adoptive father had some similarities to Hank. They were built along the same lines, except Hank carried a lot more weight than the adoptive father. Their coloring was the same, as were some of their mannerisms. The adoptive father was on the short side, and Hank was only five three. This baby would look like one of the family. But that is where the similarities ended. If there had been any personality similarities, I wouldn't have chosen this couple.

When it was all said and done, Jenny told me the couple was very impressed with me. I couldn't figure out why; I was just plain, old Chelsea. But I know I was impressed with them—not in a way that intimidated me but in a way that was right. They both had what seemed like a close walk with the Lord; they were very sensitive; they were close to their son; and they were a loving family. They had a great marriage, a great life.

I had another meeting with the adoptive parents about

three weeks later. This time I asked my good friend Clarissa to come with me. We met at a Red Lobster for dinner, and we had a wonderful time. Though Clarissa generally doesn't feel comfortable with people she doesn't know, she enjoyed herself and talked up a storm, just like she does with me. Clarissa had been one of my closest friends in all this. She walked with me when she thought I was going to get married; she had kept her opinions to herself. And she weathered the storm when I told her I was pregnant. She has had a front row seat for my growing process. We share many things. I wanted her to share this with me too.

I also wanted her to be with me when I was having the baby, though I was unwilling to ask her at first, as she has a chronic lung condition. She is often unwell and has good days and bad days. She said she'd love to be with me when I had the baby. But she had a bad spell at the end of the summer, and we knew it would be unwise for her to come. I discussed it with Georgeanne, and she said she'd come with me. Even though I had planned on her keeping the children while I was in the hospital, we were going to find a way to do both. It sounds pretty crazy, but it did work out. More on that later.

Meanwhile, some other things had been going on. It seems that I don't even have to do anything and lots of things happen to me. Some of these things are brought on by me being impulsive, and some just happen. When I was dating Hank, he nicknamed me Six Flags Over Chelsea. I'm hoping things change as I continue to grow up and slow down, but that is in the Lord's hands. Sometimes I find it hard to function if I'm not constantly dealing with things, but I'm going to try real hard to adapt to a slower pace.

Toward the end of my pregnancy, I was getting phone calls that were hang-ups. It happened more regularly as I got closer to my due date. I had the sneaking suspicion it was Hank calling to see if I was home. The phone calls mysteriously ceased as soon as Billingsly got in touch with Hank in early August, with my permission. I figure that when Hank had all the doors closed to him, he got anxious. Since he couldn't get any information about me from the pastor, I guess he felt completely in the dark. When we'd had our meeting in the pastor's office, I had mentioned adoption as an option, but at that point nothing was firm. He said he wouldn't meddle with the adoption process if it was what I wanted.

Well, Hank had his first appointment set up at Billingsly at their offices. Imagine how I felt when I found out that he wanted to look through the profile book too. Whoa, what about not meddling, Fat Boy? I was livid. He then wanted to meet the adoptive parents I had chosen. My initial reaction was not a good one. But I knew that the Lord had led me to adoption and had led me in my choice. God is not the kind of God to lead you to do something and then snatch it away. (Some might perceive God to be this way, but I don't.)

Right before Keith and Amber had their meeting with Hank, I squeezed in one more meeting. I wanted to make them aware of what to expect in that meeting. I had already sent them a letter that gave them a good feel for what to expect. I warned them of the way he could manipulate. I even went as far as to give them the option of changing their minds about the adoption altogether if they felt it could cause major problems. I told them I was willing to forgo the open adoption if it was necessary to keep Hank from having too much of a say in the raising of the child.

The meeting with Hank went well. Keith and Amber got the chance to meet the father of the baby they were about to welcome into their home as their own son. I didn't relish having the meeting and having to be so upfront with them about my involvement with Hank. But as I say, such is life.

Time both passed quickly and dragged on forever. I began to think I was going to be pregnant forever. At one point, I thought the Lord impressed on me that I would have the baby early. Sometimes I don't always hear clearly. Some things I know that I know that I know that the Lord tells me, and some things are vague. This was one of those vague things.

During the last few weeks of my pregnancy, I was becoming unglued around the edges, to put it mildly. But, of course, the day arrived—or should I say the night. It was two thirty, very early on a Tuesday morning. I'd woken up at one fifteen and couldn't sleep, so I'd decided to read, as I was wont to do when sleepless. I'd started noticing things going on in my body even then but decided I was going to ignore them. They didn't stop, so I thought I might start timing things.

When two thirty rolled around, there was no doubting and no ignoring. This was for real, and the contractions were coming extremely close together. I waited until three to call Georgeanne. She showed up shortly afterward. Meanwhile I was kind of walking around, trying to get last-minute things packed. When she arrived, the contractions were four minutes apart and getting closer.

I called Ainsley to see if she could come over and get the

boys off to school a little later in the morning. No problem. Georgeanne could see I was kind of going around in circles and said, "We're leaving. Tell Ainsley we'll leave the door open." We went about two miles down the road, and I realized I'd left my Medicaid papers at home.

We arrived at the hospital at four thirty. They wouldn't let me go to the room until I checked in. Yes, I had procrastinated on sending in my admission papers. By the time I got to the labor and delivery room, it was five. Things were moving along rapidly. I was five centimeters. At 6:33 a.m., my baby boy was born. The labor had been intense and painful, but the pain was bearable. I had prayed that the Lord would make it bearable, and of course He had come through again.

There is nothing to describe the joyous feeling I had as I held that sweet little baby to my bosom minutes after birth.

26
Good-Bye

I had decided to room with my son. This was my time with him, never to be forgotten. It would be like storing up jewels in a treasure chest to be taken out and admired. Now this memory is one of my treasures to look at over the years. He was such a good baby in the room with me.

It was a while before I was settled into my room, and they had baby things to do with him in the nursery. When they brought him into the room, he was all cleaned up and bundled in a little shirt. I fed him throughout the day and changed his diaper. I would just look over, and there he was.

Time flew. Of course, I spent a lot of time on the phone, telling people the wonderful news. Late that night, at around one, I was lying in bed thinking about my little boy and remembering what the Lord had brought me through and led me to. Some thoughts nibbled at the edge of my mind: *How can you leave here without this baby? What's wrong with you?* I knew immediately who the author of those thoughts was and rejected them.

At that time, the door opened. I thought it must be time to feed the baby again. A nurse came into my room and stood there silently at the base of the baby's bed for a moment. She then called me by my name and told me that the choice I had made was a wonderful thing and that I had no idea how many people it would impact—not just adoptive parents, but grandparents, uncles, aunts, and many more. She told me she was an adoptive grandparent and how her daughter had lost three babies in the fifth month of her pregnancy. She poured out her heart to me. This was just another thing to add to my treasure chest. I will never forget how God so graciously provided for me in that crucial moment of need.

Amber called me the next day. I told her, "This was for real. You'll see your baby, and he's beautiful." I had wanted them to come and see us in the hospital, but they couldn't do it. I understood, though I was a bit disappointed.

The time had come. Georgeanne said she would be down the hall in the waiting room. It was my time to say good-bye. As I held the baby in my arms one last time, I knew the moment I had put off had arrived. I told him that I loved him and that I wanted so much to bring him home with me to be a part of my family with Luke and Eli. But I wanted him to have more than I could offer. I could give him all the love in the world, but I couldn't give him a complete family.

I looked at his sweet body resting in my arms and realized the time had come. God created in us women a deep maternal instinct that is impossible to deny, and then He created babies, helpless little bundles of sweetness that depend on us, their mothers, for everything. And that is why He made humans that way, so we could bond. My bonding with my baby was over; it was time for him to bond with his new family. I carried him for nine months and had those hours with him there. But it was time for him to bond with those that would give him so much more. I loved my son, and I said good-bye.

God is merciful. In all this He has brought about so many changes in my life. I've finally grown up. I no longer want to look for people to fill my needs, but to the Lord. And one of the best things is the work He has built on the foundation He laid with my two sons. I've always loved my boys, but somehow I just couldn't get very far in this. God has given me more love for them than I ever knew. I enjoy them so much more. I have so much to give them. I look at them with different eyes. I have a new beginning ready for God to build upon.

Many people would look at my circumstances and stand in judgment or pity. Very few people could understand why I would make an adoption plan, but that's not the important thing. It's what God thinks that matters. Others might say, "What a horrible thing to have to go through." Satan tried his hardest to make it that way for me. I didn't always go about with joy and triumph; there were many times I felt horrible about myself. But I don't want to base my walk with the Lord on my feelings; they often betray me. I base it on what He tells me in His Word, and that's that He loves me more than I can begin to imagine. I can honestly say that I'm glad all this happened to me. It has brought about so many wonderful things.

Life does go on. And the pain lessens. There are times when it's hard. That's when I remind myself of the wonderful life this child now has and will have. And I look at my own sons and know that God will provide me with all I need for them. I sure am looking forward to enjoying a slower pace. Maybe it's time to put Six Flags Over Chelsea to rest.

www.ingramcontent.com/pod-product-compliance
Lightning Source LLC
Chambersburg PA
CBHW071456070526
44578CB00001B/365